# PLANT BASED COOKBOOK FOR BEGINNERS

Green Gourmet: Elevate Your Health, Thrive on Plants - A Beginner's Guide to Plant-Powered Palate Pleasures

ANTHONY FERGUSON

# TABLE OF CONTENTS

# Introduction

Imagine a world where vibrant flavors dance across your palate, nourishing your body and soul with every bite. Welcome to the captivating realm of plant-based cuisine, a culinary adventure that celebrates the incredible diversity and abundance of nature's bounty. Whether you're embarking on a journey towards a healthier lifestyle, embracing ethical choices, or simply seeking to expand your culinary horizons, this book is your ultimate guide to unlocking the delicious and nourishing potential of plant-based foods.

In the pages that follow, you'll discover a treasure trove of mouth-watering recipes that will redefine your understanding of plant-based cuisine. From wholesome and energizing breakfasts to hearty and satisfying mains, from vibrant salads and soups to decadent sweet treats, this book has something to delight every palate. But this isn't just a collection of recipes; it's a comprehensive roadmap that will empower you to navigate the plant-based world with confidence and ease.

Explore the many benefits of a plant-based diet, from its positive impact on your health and well-being to its environmental sustainability and ethical considerations. Dispel common myths and misconceptions, and gain a deeper understanding of how to thrive on a plant-powered regimen. Learn the art of stocking a well-equipped plant-based pantry, mastering essential kitchen tools and techniques, and understanding the fundamentals of plant-based nutrition.

Whether you're a curious newcomer or a seasoned plant-based enthusiast, this book is your ultimate companion on a journey towards a more vibrant, conscious, and delicious way of life. Embrace the abundance of nature's gifts, and let your taste buds embark on an extraordinary adventure that will elevate your health, ignite your culinary creativity, and delight your senses like never before.

Get ready to embark on a flavorful and fulfilling odyssey, where every bite is a celebration of the plant-based lifestyle. Welcome to the "Green Gourmet" – a world where nourishment and indulgence harmoniously converge, and where every meal is a testament to the power of plants to tantalize and satisfy.

# Chapter 1

# Introduction to Plant-Based Eating

### Why plant-based eating?

There has been a seismic shift in the way many people view food and nutrition over the past decade. The plant-based diet, which emphasizes deriving nutrients from fruits, vegetables, whole grains, legumes, nuts, and seeds, has skyrocketed in popularity. While this way of eating isn't an entirely new concept, the recent surge in interest has brought plant-based diets into the mainstream consciousness. But what's really behind this movement? Why are people increasingly choosing to eat more plants and fewer animal products? The reasons are multifaceted and compelling.

- **Health Benefits of Plant-Based Eating**

From a health perspective, study after study has demonstrated the numerous benefits of following a plant-rich diet. Consuming more plant foods and fewer animal products is consistently associated with a lower risk of numerous chronic diseases, including heart disease, type 2 diabetes, certain cancers, and obesity.

The evidence is crystal clear that plant-based diets are great for cardiovascular health. They tend to be low in saturated fat and cholesterol while supplying the body with high levels of fiber, antioxidants, and beneficial plant compounds - a combination that helps reduce inflammation, improves cholesterol levels, and maintains healthy blood pressure. The landmark Nurses' Health Study, which tracked over 120,000 people for decades, found that those who adhered closest to a plant-based diet had a significantly lower risk of developing heart disease.

Type 2 diabetes has reached epidemic proportions worldwide, but plant-based diets may help combat this growing crisis. Research shows that these eating patterns can improve insulin sensitivity and reduce the risk of developing diabetes. In one major study, those following a low-fat vegan diet experienced improved blood sugar control and required less medication compared to a control group on a standard diabetes diet. Plant foods are packed with fiber which slows the absorption of sugars, and many are low on the glycemic index, meaning they have little impact on blood sugar levels.

There are also intriguing links between plant-based diets and cancer prevention. Plant foods are rich in phytochemicals, biologically active compounds that may protect cells from the types of damage that can initiate cancer. Large-scale studies have found that vegetarians have modestly lower rates of cancer incidence overall. And diets centered around plants may be especially helpful for reducing the risk of certain cancers like breast, prostate, and colon cancer. More research is still needed, but the findings are promising.

The battle against obesity is another area where plant-based diets may offer solutions. Since plant foods tend to be high in fiber and nutrient-dense, they can promote feelings of fullness and satiety. This makes it easier to consume fewer calories without feeling deprived. Vegan and vegetarian diets have been shown to facilitate weight loss while also reducing obesity-related health markers like high cholesterol and blood pressure.

Beyond the potential to prevent and help manage disease, plant-based eating patterns may also promote longevity. Fascinating research on Blue Zones - regions with a high proportion of centenarians - reveals that diets consisting mainly of unprocessed plant foods are common among these long-lived populations. And the largest study to date on vegetarians and vegans found that these groups had a lower overall mortality rate compared to those consuming meat.

- **Ethical Considerations**

While the health benefits alone are compelling, many people choose a plant-based lifestyle for ethical reasons related to reducing animal suffering and demonstrating environmental stewardship.

From a compassionate standpoint, eliminating animal products from one's diet prevents the exploitation, maltreatment, and slaughter of farm animals raised for food. Even under the best of circumstances, industrialized animal agriculture requires that living, sentient beings be forced into confinement and ultimately killed – a reality that troubles many people on moral grounds. For those concerned about animal welfare, plant-based eating provides an ethical alternative.

Additionally, there are significant environmental costs associated with animal agriculture. Raising animals for food is a highly resource-intensive process that requires immense amounts of land, water, and crops to sustain. The United Nations has declared that animal agriculture accounts for more greenhouse gas emissions than all forms of transportation combined. Given the existential threat of climate change and environmental degradation, many feel that a shift toward plant-based eating is a critical part of the solution.

- **The Allure of Plant-Based Eating**

Beyond the substantial health benefits and ethical motivations, plant-based eating is attracting interest for its sheer culinary allure. Across the globe, chefs are showcasing the incredible versatility, vibrant flavors, and aesthetic appeal of plant foods through innovative cuisine. Fine dining establishments are introducing sumptuous plant-based tasting menus to rave reviews. Home cooks have unprecedented access to creative, internationally-inspired recipes thanks to popular blogs, social media, cookbooks, and online resources.

As the options have expanded, it's become easier to maintain interest and avoid food boredom with plant-based eating. Not long ago, the mere concept of a "vegan restaurant" was quirky at best. Now, you can find plant-based burgers, pizza, tacos, sushi, and even delectable cheeses made entirely from plant ingredients in most major cities. Innovative food technology and culinary craftsmanship are ensuring that plant-based eaters never have to compromise on flavor or satisfaction.

The momentum behind plant-based eating shows no signs of slowing down anytime soon. The scientific evidence continues to mount underscoring the health advantages of diets centered around minimally-processed plant foods. Millions of people are embracing this way of eating as an ethical, environmentally-friendly choice. And innovative chefs and food companies are tapping into the growing appetite for plant-based fare that is both delicious and sustainable.

For those looking to improve their health, reduce their environmental impact, avoid contributing to animal suffering, experience new culinary frontiers, or some combination thereof – plant-based eating offers an appealing path forward. Whether strictly vegan or a more flexible vegetarian or plant-based diet, increasing one's intake of whole plant foods is something that can benefit us all.

**Benefits of a plant-based diet**

What you eat forms the building blocks of your body. The foods you consume quite literally become you, providing the nutrients and compounds that comprise your cells, fuel your energy, and determine how your biological systems function. Given the vital importance of diet, it's no surprise that there is so much interest and debate around what constitutes optimal nutrition for human health. While opinions may differ, the evidence is mounting that a plant-based diet - one centered around fruits, vegetables, whole grains, legumes, nuts, and seeds - offers tremendous benefits spanning physical health, disease prevention, environmental impact, and beyond. Here's a look at why eating more plants is an wise choice.

- **Promoting Overall Health**

Numerous studies have demonstrated that plant-based diets are associated with better overall health metrics compared to diets rich in animal products. Those following plant-based eating patterns tend to have lower rates of obesity, reduced risks for heart disease and diabetes, improved cholesterol and blood pressure numbers, and lower inflammation levels. This superior metabolic health profile stems from the nutrient-density and favorable composition of plant foods.

Plants provide exceptionally high levels of fiber, antioxidants, beneficial plant compounds like phytochemicals and phytonutrients, and healthy unsaturated fats. At the same time, minimally processed plant foods are naturally low in saturated fat, cholesterol, added sugars, and other compounds that can contribute to poor health when consumed in excess. This combination helps support ideal weight, robust cardiovascular function, effective regulation of blood sugar, and lower systematic inflammation.

Research also points to longevity benefits associated with plant-based eating. Population studies have found vegetarians and vegans tend to live longer than those consuming meat regularly. The Adventist Health Study, which followed thousands of individuals for decades, is a prime example – vegetarians had a 12% lower risk of death over the study period. Data from Blue Zones, areas with an exceptional number of centenarians, also reveals plant-centric diets as a common lifestyle factor among the longest-lived populations.

While plant-based certainly doesn't equate to deprivation, these diets do promote a dietary pattern of plentiful whole, unprocessed plant foods and reduced intake of calorie-dense processed fare and animal products high in saturated fat, cholesterol, and preservatives. This emphasis on nutrient-rich, high-fiber foods makes it easier to maintain an ideal weight, prevent nutrient deficiencies, lower chronic disease risk, and simply feel your physical best.

- **Mitigating Disease Risk**

In addition to the general health-promoting properties of plant-based diets, the research reveals compelling links between plant-centric eating and reduced incidence of some of the most serious chronic diseases like heart disease, type 2 diabetes, and even certain forms of cancer.

Cardiovascular disease is a leading cause of death and disability worldwide, but plant-based diets have been shown to be highly effective for both prevention and, in some cases, even reversal of heart disease. A low-fat, plant-based dietary pattern has been demonstrated to open up clogged coronary arteries by promoting better cholesterol levels, improved blood pressure, and reduced inflammation – key drivers of atherosclerosis.

Study after study shows that plant-based eaters have a significantly lower risk of developing type 2 diabetes compared to non-vegetarians. Since obesity is a major risk factor for diabetes, the tendency toward lower weight among plant-based individuals helps explain part of the protective effect. But even when you control for Body Mass Index (BMI), the benefits persist, thanks to enhanced insulin sensitivity stemming from the high fiber intake and favorable nutrient composition of plants.

While more research is still needed, mounting evidence suggests plant-forward eating may reduce cancer risk as well, particularly for certain forms like breast, prostate, and colon cancers. Plant foods are dense in antioxidants and phytochemicals that can protect cells from the types of damage that initiate cancer. Large cohort studies have found vegetarians and vegans tend to have modestly lower overall cancer rates. It's an intriguing and active area of investigation.

- **Environmental Stewardship**

In addition to human health, there are compelling reasons to adopt a plant-based diet from an environmental perspective. The statistics on the strain that animal agriculture places on the world's natural resources are startling. According to comprehensive research conducted by the Food and Agriculture Organization of the United Nations (FAO), animal agriculture is a major driver of greenhouse gas emissions, land degradation, deforestation, water pollution, species extinction, and other environmental impacts.

Animal agriculture accounts for up to 18% of total human-caused greenhouse gas emissions – a staggering volume exceeding even the transportation sector's contribution. Thanks to activities like clearing land for grazing and feed production, raising livestock is also a leading cause of deforestation, natural habitat destruction, species loss, and erosion of topsoil. It takes 10 pounds of plant protein to produce just 1 pound of animal protein for human consumption. And animal waste runoff from farms is a significant source of water pollution globally.

By simply shifting toward a more plant-centric dietary pattern, individuals can dramatically reduce their environmental impact and mitigate the ecological toll associated with industrial-scale animal agriculture. It's a prudent choice for those concerned about climate change, sustainability, and preserving the planet's precious biodiversity and natural resources for future generations.

- **Abundant Flavors and Culinary Exploration**

Perceptions around plant-based eating have evolved dramatically in recent years. Gone are the stereotypical notions of bland, boring vegan food consisting of little more than simple vegetables, fruits, and grains. Today, there is an appreciation and enthusiasm surrounding the rich diversity, culinary artistry, and sheer deliciousness possible when cooking with the full, vibrant spectrum of plant-based ingredients.

Thanks to creative recipe developers, chefs, food blogs, magazines, and other educational resources, it's easier than ever to enjoy phenomenal vegan cuisine spanning global culinary traditions. Lively flavors, satisfying textures, and elegant presentations rival the finest non-vegan offerings. Plant-based chefs are elevating foods like legumes, grains, fresh produce, nuts, and seeds into delectable entrees, snacks, baked goods, desserts, and everything in between.

Major cities now boast thriving vegan food scenes with exceptional plant-based taquerias, burger joints, pan-Asian eateries, pizza shops, and fine dining establishments. Food technology is also fueling an innovation boom resulting in high-quality plant-based meat and dairy alternatives for those seeking the familiar tastes and textures of animal products. All of this has made plant-based eating exciting, varied, and appealing to both longtime vegans and those simply aiming to incorporate more plant foods into their routine.

- **Making the Transition**

While the benefits of plant-based eating are compelling from health, environmental, ethical, and culinary perspectives, making the transition is still a major lifestyle change for most people. Some find it helpful to shift incrementally by first adopting a vegetarian diet and then potentially moving toward a fully plant-based vegan approach. Others prefer diving in headfirst by immediately eliminating animal products from their routine.

There can certainly be a learning curve when it comes to mastering plant-based cooking skills, menu planning, dining out, supplementing nutrients like vitamin B12, and addressing social situations or family dynamics. However, there are now extensive resources ranging from cookbooks and blogs to community support groups and health coaching services to help ease the transition. With determination, preparation, and an appreciation for the many benefits of plant-based eating, the commitment becomes rewarding rather than restricting.

- **The Momentum Builds**

  With notable individuals like elite athletes, celebrities, and influential entrepreneurs increasingly vocal about their plant-based lifestyles, the diet continues gaining momentum across the globe. Fast food and casual dining chains are rapidly expanding their plant-based menus to satisfy growing consumer demand. Educational materials on plant-based eating are now commonly found in settings like physicians' offices and workplace wellness programs.

Well-designed research continues yielding insights into the benefits of plant-based diets for disease prevention, management of conditions like diabetes, healthy weight maintenance, longevity, and more. Professional medical organizations like the American College of Cardiology are endorsing plant-based eating patterns as part of their guidance for preventing and treating heart disease, diabetes, obesity, and other chronic illnesses.

The plant-based movement shows no signs of slowing its ascent. As consumer interest grows alongside the compelling scientific evidence and success stories, a profound dietary shift appears to be taking hold for good reason.

- **The Case for Plant-Based Eating**

  Given the myriad benefits associated with eating a predominantly plant-based diet, it's no wonder the movement is surging in popularity. The advantages for personal health are extensive, spanning everything from general wellness and disease prevention to healthy weight management and longevity.

  Plants are nutrient-dense powerhouses supplying high levels of fiber, antioxidants, beneficial compounds, and healthy fats while being low in compounds that can contribute to disease. It's an optimal nutritional package that promotes ideal body weight, robust heart health, effective blood sugar regulation, and lower inflammation.

Compelling research links plant-centric diets to substantially lower risks for some of the most pernicious chronic diseases including heart disease, diabetes, and certain cancers. For those already facing these conditions, thoughtfully planned plant-based eating can be a powerful tool for prevention, management, or even reversal.

Perhaps most critically in our modern era, plant-based diets allow people to dramatically reduce their environmental footprint by minimizing participation in the highly resource-intensive and ecologically damaging industrial animal agriculture system. Adopting a more plant-based lifestyle is an ethical choice to avoid directly contributing to institutionalized animal cruelty and suffering as well.

Once dismissed as bland or limiting, modern plant-based cuisine showcases the incredible versatility, global culinary inspiration, and delectable flavors possible when talented chefs harness the full spectrum of whole plant ingredients. It's food that nourishes both body and soul.

Whether people adopt a plant-based diet for their health, the planet, moral considerations, or simply the joy of eating wonderful plant-derived fare, the movement has never been more vibrant or supported by robust evidence. While no one way of eating is perfect for everyone, the case for increasing one's intake of whole plant foods is compelling indeed. It's a path well worth exploring for all it has to offer.

**Dispelling myths and misconceptions**

As plant-based diets have surged in popularity, so too have the myths and misconceptions surrounding this way of eating. From concerns about getting enough protein to claims that plant-based is just another fad diet, there's no shortage of misinformation circulating. But many of these notions simply don't hold up to scrutiny when you examine the full body of scientific evidence and the reality of what plant-based eating entails. Let's separate fact from fiction and dispel some of the most common myths.

- **Myth: Plant-Based Diets Are Deficient in Protein**

This is likely the most pervasive myth surrounding plant-based diets – the misguided belief that removing animal products from your routine will leave you lacking in protein. The reality is that getting adequate protein from plants is straightforward and readily achievable for anyone willing to incorporate a sensible variety of foods into their diet.

Plentiful plant-based protein sources include legumes (beans, lentils, peas), whole grains, nuts, seeds, and even vegetables like broccoli, spinach and Brussels sprouts contain some protein. Soy-based foods like tofu, tempeh and edamame are particularly protein-rich plant options. With a balanced, well-planned routine, it's easy for vegans and vegetarians to meet their protein needs without any animal products.

The key lies in eating enough calorie-dense protein sources and varying your intake from different plant foods throughout the day. For instance, a day of plant-based eating could include oatmeal with nuts and seeds for breakfast, a lentil and vegetable-based soup for lunch, and a grain bowl with tofu and beans for dinner. Simple snacks like hummus and veggies or trail mix help round out protein intake.

Numerous studies have analyzed protein intake and status among vegans and vegetarians, consistently showing they meet requirements just as readily as non-vegetarians. As long as calorie needs are met and there's variation in the diet, plant protein deficiency is simply a non-issue for the vast majority.

Myth: You Can't Get Enough Nutrients Without Animal Products

Another common myth is that eliminating animal products like meat, eggs and dairy from your diet will render you woefully deficient in key vitamins and nutrients. But again, this broad claim doesn't align with the reality of a balanced, well-planned plant-based diet.

While it's certainly possible to construct a nutrient-deficient diet from plant foods alone, it's just as possible to construct an unhealthy diet containing animal products. Nutritional deficiencies stem from poor meal planning and lack of variety – not strictly from the absence or inclusion of animal products.

Plants offer more than enough of every essential vitamin and mineral humans need when eaten in strategic combinations. Many plant foods like leafy greens, beans, nuts, and seeds provide impressive amounts of nutrients like iron, calcium, zinc, vitamin B12, and vitamin D that some people wrongly assume can only come from animal-based sources. With smart meal planning and supplementation where prudent, plant-based diets can absolutely cover all nutrient needs.

In fact, research suggests those following plant-based diets have a lower risk of certain nutrient deficiencies compared to the general population, as plant-centric meals promote higher intakes of fiber, antioxidants, phytochemicals, and other health-promoting components that many omnivore diets lack.

- **Myth: Plant-Based Eating is Just a Fad Diet**

  While plant-based lifestyles may be gaining more widespread popularity in recent years, the concept of deriving one's nutrition from plant sources is hardly a fad. Cultures around the globe have centuries of history following plant-based ways of eating rooted in ethical, spiritual, environmental or health-driven belief systems.

Many ancient civilizations like those in Greece, India and parts of the ancient Mediterranean world subscribed to philosophies promoting plant-based diets linked to nonviolence, discipline, physical vitality and living in harmony with nature. These concepts laid the foundation for modern vegan and vegetarian traditions that still continue today.

Far from just a fleeting dietary trend, the plant-based movement we're experiencing today is an extension and evolution of a tradition spanning millennia. Rather than a fad, plant-based eating represents a renaissance and growing mainstream awareness of ethical and health principles that predate recorded history.

The irrefutable evidence on the health and environmental benefits of plant-centric diets will further cement their staying power as a permanent movement, not just another weight-loss fad. Humanity is rediscovering the wisdom of our plant-eating ancestors and synthesizing it with modern nutritional science and culinary innovation. This is a paradigm shift, not a passing craze.

- **Myth: Plant-Based Eating is Inconvenient and Limiting**

For those accustomed to the standard Western diet rich in meat, dairy, eggs and processed foods, the prospect of eliminating all animal products can seem daunting, inconvenient or overly restrictive at first glance. But in reality, plant-based cuisine is remarkably versatile, flavorful and satisfying when you approach it with an open mind.

From hearty stews, curries and chilis to decadent baked goods, burgers and other handhelds, nourishing bowls and salads, vegan and vegetarian fare can be every bit as convenient, varied and crave-worthy as the familiar meat-centric meals many grow up eating. They're simply built around different ingredient combinations and culinary traditions.

The plant-based lifestyle isn't about deprivation, it's about culinary creativity and conscious consumption of whole, nutritious plant foods. Meal prepping, using the freezer, keeping staple ingredients stocked, and learning some basic plant-based cooking methods can make eating this way remarkably easy and anything but limiting.

There are now innumerable blogs, social media accounts, cookbooks, and other resources offering endlessly creative and delicious plant-based recipe inspiration spanning global cuisines. Not to mention, the restaurant industry has caught up with a growing number of dedicated vegan and vegetarian eateries popping up in most major cities.

What was once considered niche and restrictive has gone completely mainstream, with more enticing options than ever before to enjoy an immensely varied plant-based culinary experience.

- **Myth: You'll Never Feel Satisfied Eating Only Plants**

  This myth likely stems from assumptions that vegan foods are meager salads and side dishes rather than hearty, satisfying meals built around nutrient-dense ingredients like whole grains, nuts, seeds and legumes. There's also a misconception that the complete absence of animal products like meat inherently leaves you feeling unsatisfied.

The truth is, against all stereotypes, plant-based meals are incredibly satiating thanks to the fiber, protein and healthy fats they contain. Dishes like high-protein lentil pastas, grain bowls loaded with crispy tofu and roasted veggies, creamy nut-based curries or bean-based chilis deliver immense flavor and sustenance from a variety of plant sources.

The key is getting adequate calories from nutrient-dense whole plant foods rather than over-relying on refined carbs or fats, which can leave you feeling unsatisfied. But a properly constructed plant-based meal should leave you feeling pleasantly full for hours.

What's more, many plant-based meat and dairy alternatives like veggie burgers, nut-based cheeses, and soy milks are remarkably satisfying in their texture and flavors while being completely plant-derived. With countless ways to craft hearty, wholesome meals packed with plant proteins and healthy fats, plant-based eating is supremely satisfying and anything but deprivation.

- **Looking Past the Myths**

While the misconceptions around plant-based diets are numerous, many stem from a fundamental lack of understanding about what this way of eating truly entails. By simply educating oneself on the basics of plant-based nutrition and meal construction, most of the misguided concerns quickly evaporate into myth-busting realities.

Plant-based diets adhere to sound principles of nutrition while offering incredible versatility, convenience, and exciting culinary exploration. Rather than limiting or depriving, plant-based eating opens up a new world of flavors, textures, and globally-inspired ingredient combinations. It's a lifestyle rooted in centuries of tradition while featuring modern innovations that shatter any notions of restrictive, boring food.

With their potential to promote personal health, environmental sustainability, and ethical eating principles that align with many people's values, plant-centric diets have earned their rightful place in today's mainstream. Stripping away the myths allows the benefits of this powerful way of eating to shine through, setting us up to make informed, well-reasoned decisions about the food we choose to fuel us.

# Chapter 2

# Getting Started

## Stocking a plant-based pantry

- **Stocking Your Plant-Based Pantry: A Guide to Culinary Abundance**

The pantry forms the foundation of any well-stocked kitchen. It's where we keep our essential dry goods, shelf-stable ingredients, and cooking staples designed for long-term storage. For plant-based eaters, curating the perfect plant-stocked pantry allows us to craft delicious, nutritious meals drawing upon a diverse array of flavors, textures, and global culinary traditions.

With a few key categories covered and some basic planning, you can transform your pantry into the ideal headquarters for your plant-based kitchen adventures. Let's explore the essential elements so you'll always have those crucial ingredients on hand to turn out satisfying vegan fare with ease.

- **Grains and Starches: The Versatile Staples**

  When browsing the vast expanse of plant-derived ingredients out there, a great place to start is with hearty whole grains and starches. These affordable, endlessly versatile foundations allow you to construct all sorts of delicious plant-based meals.

Start by keeping supplies of brown rice, quinoa, oats, whole wheat pasta, bread, tortillas, and crackers. Venture further afield with other spectacular whole grains like farro, freekeh, millet, barley, corn, buckwheat, and teff. These ancient grains can elevate plant-based dishes while providing essential nutrients like fiber, protein, and minerals.

For a serious pantry boost, explore more unique starches and flour alternatives. Stocking items like potatoes, sweet potatoes, cassava root and plantains allows for creative dishes spanning morning hash to baked goods and warming stews. Gluten-free flours like chickpea, almond, coconut, and oat flour introduce even more possibilities.

With such an abundant variety of shelf-stable grains, seeds, and roots to draw upon, you'll never lack for hearty, satisfying plant-based meal foundations. Whole grains alone offer seemingly endless versatility to create everything from morning porridges and veggie burgers to pilafs, grain bowls and so much more.

- **The Protein-Packed Pantry Heroes: Legumes and Pulses**

Speaking of plant-based protein sources, one would be remiss without dedicating serious pantry real estate to a lavish supply of lentils, beans, peas, and their leguminous cousins. These protein-packed superfoods offer incredible culinary versatility while forming the backbone of many traditional dishes from cultures around the globe.

A well-stocked plant-based pantry includes dried chickpeas, lentils, black beans, pinto beans, kidney beans, and split peas at an absolute minimum. But expanding your horizons with unique varieties like adzuki beans, black-eyed peas, mung beans, fava beans, and green lentils pays off with incredible flavor and textural diversity.

To save time, it's also wise to keep plenty of canned and precooked legumes on hand as well. Options like chickpeas, black beans, and lentils simply can't be beat for their convenience and ease of use in creating quick plant-based meals and snacks. Don't forget shelf-stable soy foods like tofu, tempeh, and edamame either – they're all protein-packed all-stars.

With the right legume reserves fully stocked, you'll have a wealth of nutritious plant-based protein to draw upon for everything from sumptuous curries, stews, soups and chilies to dips, salads, burgers and so much more.

- **The Functional Pantry Enhancers**

To take the flavors and nutrient-density of your plant-based dishes to soaring heights, be sure to incorporate a collection of functional and flavorful enhancers into your pantry stockpile. These are the sorts of shelf-stable ingredients that instantly elevate even the simplest plant-based recipes with zest, richness, and nutrition.

In the dried spice and herb department, build an arsenal of versatile seasonings like chili powder, garam masala, curry powder, dried basil, thyme, oregano, smoked paprika, cumin, and cinnamon. These will embolden your veggie sautés, stews, curries and just about any savory plant-based cooking with delightful aromatics and pizzazz.

Complementary dry goods like tomato paste, vegetable stock cubes, and coconut milk add richness and depth of flavor while introducing valuable nutrients like healthy fats and minerals. Fermented foods like soy sauce, miso, vinegars, nutritional yeast and vegan Worcestershire sauce work wonders to infuse an umami burst into plant-based meals.

Meanwhile, nuts, seeds, and dried fruits form all-star flavor enhancers and crunchy nutritious toppings. Keep supplies of walnuts, almonds, cashews, pistachios, pumpkin seeds, sunflower seeds, chia seeds, and dried cranberries, cherries, dates or apricots stocked at all times. Adding a sprinkle here or crumble there delivers texture and a boost of protective plant compounds.

- **The Flavor-Packed Condiments, Sauces and Oils**

Prepared condiments, sauces and oils will become your dearest plant-based pantry friends when it comes to imparting bold lip-smacking flavors to any culinary creation. With a versatile arsenal of these ready-to-use ingredients at your fingertips, you can transform even the humblest plant ingredients into vibrant feasts for the senses.

Having multipurpose oils like olive, avocado, toasted sesame, and coconut oils in your pantry empowers you to sauté, roast, drizzle and dress with abandon. These plant-based oils bring distinctive richness and flavors to all styles of cuisine. The right oil can make or break a plant-based dish.

Stock up on savory, creamy and sweet plant-based sauces to build sauces, dips, dressings and glazes upon. Items like nut and seed butters, dairy-free creams, fruit purees, chutneys, salsas, dairy-free cheese sauces, and international condiments make meal prepping a breeze while lending signature flavors.

For example, smooth almond butter features in rich curries, cashew cream stars in sumptuous Alfredo sauces, zesty fruit chutneys make magical toppings for grain bowls or porridges, and a quality vegan ranch dressing elevates even the simplest veggie crudités or slaws. With the right saucy stockpile, you'll always have options for plant-based meals brimming with pizzazz.

- **The Pantry Wrapped Up**

Truthfully, there is no limit to the ingredients one can stock and celebrate in a plant-based kitchen Romancing flavors, textures, and culinary cultural traditions allows you to explore plant-based eating through an endlessly expansive and exciting lens. However, ensuring your pantry contains a solid foundation of essentials is key.

From wholesome whole grains and legumes to a vibrant collection of herbs, spices, nuts, seeds and other flavorful enhancers, the plant-based pantry offers a remarkable canvas for crafting nourishing and inventive chef-worthy creations in the kitchen. Build out your inventory of shelf-stable plant staples and you'll be equipped to make nutritious and deeply satisfying plant-based meals at a moment's notice.

The plant-based lifestyle celebrates exploration, variety, and cherishing nature's boundless culinary gifts. By thoughtfully stocking your plant-powered pantry, you'll set the stage for vibrant, wholesome, and effortlessly delicious plant-based eating to become a joyous daily ritual. Few things are more rewarding than creating magnificent plant-based feasts from a well-equipped kitchen bounty. Get stocking and discover for yourself.

## Essential kitchen tools and equipment

For the plant-based cook, the kitchen is a canvas upon which culinary magic happens. From simmering up an aromatic lentil stew to baking a batch of supremely fudgy vegan brownies, preparing vibrant whole food, plant-based fare requires the right tools for the job.

Just as a painter needs a well-stocked arsenal of brushes, paints, and canvases to bring their vision to life, so too does the vegan chef rely on an assortment of kitchen tools and equipment to execute their plant-powered feasts with efficiency and flair. Let's explore some of the essential workhorses you'll want in your kitchen corner for streamlined plant-based meal prep.

- **The Versatile Virtuosos: Knives and Cutting Boards**

For any chef worth their salt, a high-quality set of knives will be their most prized and frequently used kitchen workhorses. When it comes to plant-based cooking, chances are you'll be doing lots of slicing, dicing, mincing, and chopping given the fresh produce-heavy nature of the cuisine. That's why it pays to invest in a versatile set of razor-sharp knives designed to make quick work of all your fruit and vegetable prep needs.

At minimum, aim to have a large chef's knife, a serrated bread knife, and a paring knife in your knife block. For next-level efficiency, you may also want a santoku knife for precision tasks, kitchen shears for snipping herbs, and even a mandoline-style slicer for rapidly prepping veggies like carrots and potatoes. Keeping your knives razor-sharp is key, which is why a honing steel or electric sharpener deserves a spot in your kitchen toolkit.

You'll want to pair those gleaming knives with an equally high-performing set of cutting boards. Invest in a few large wood or bamboo boards that won't dull your blade edges. Having multiple boards lets you easily segregate ingredients and clean up between tasks. For quick veggie chopping jobs, a secure non-slip board can be hugely helpful.

With a premium set of cutlery and boards built for efficient food prep, you'll make swift work of transforming all those fresh fruits, veggies, and plant ingredients into gorgeous platters, snacks, and main dishes. They're the versatile virtuosos no plant-based cook should be without.

- **The Power Couple: Food Processor and High-Speed Blender**

Nowadays, most kitchens are outfitted with a powerful food processor or high-speed blender counterpart. For those whipping up plant-based delights, having both of these appliances is absolutely essential for streamlining recipes and opening up a world of new culinary possibilities.

A food processor is a true multitasking marvel that allows you to quickly shred, chop, mince, grind, mix, knead and even make nut butters from scratch out of whole foods. Processors equip you to blitz up chickpea falafels, nut-based cheeze sauces, seed-based "tuna" salads, healthy hummus, and so much more with ease. For sauces, dips, patties, and veggie-packed dishes where you need a coarse or finely chopped texture, the food processor is your best friend.

On the other hand, a high-powered blender like a Vitamix or Blendtec gives you the ability to puree batters, dough, smoothies, and sauces into exceptionally smooth and creamy textures. Thick shakes, fresh nut milks, dressings, sweet puddings, and rich bisques all become easily executable with this mighty appliance. The intense motor and blade design can even handle grinding grains into flour with ease.

While it's certainly possible to get by without these gadgets, having both a quality food processor and high-speed blender on your countertop allows you to fully unlock the potential of countless plant-based recipes. Together they form a dynamic duo no plant-based kitchen should be without.

- **The Batch Cookers: Slow Cooker, Instant Pot, and Sheet Pans**

  One of the brilliant aspects of plant-based cooking is that many dishes actually develop richer, more satisfying flavors when the ingredients have time to slowly commingle over gentle heat. That's where batch cooking appliances like a slow cooker, Instant Pot multi-cooker, and reliable sheet pans come into play. These humble workhorses allow you to easily prepare large volumes of plant-based staples to enjoy throughout the week.

While slow cookers impart their signature rich, concentrated flavors to vegan stews, chilis, curries, beans, and sauces over a long gentle simmer, multi-cookers like the Instant Pot combine those slow cooking abilities with pressure cooking technology that can slash cooking times dramatically. Both are perfect for simmering up big batches of bean dishes, soups, sauces, grains, and even dairy-free yogurt with ease.

Meanwhile, sturdy sheet pans are indispensable for roasting larger quantities of vegetables, tofu, chickpeas, fries, and other hearty plant-based basics. Lining up baking trays in the oven lets you roast enough delicious plant food to enjoy as meal components or snacks throughout the week ahead. They're true batch cooking saviors.

With a few well-used cookers and oven sheets incorporated into your weekly meal prep routine, you'll have a constant supply of delicious, ready-to-go wholesome plant-based ingredients on hand to mix and match into quick meals. For modern vegan eating, these batch cookers empower a level of convenience that cements this lifestyle for the long haul.

- **The Mod Essentials: Air Fryers, Immersion Blenders and Spiralizers**

While not necessarily kitchen must-haves, there are some modern innovative appliances and tools that can supercharge your plant-based cooking experience with exciting new flavors and techniques. For those plant-eaters who love to experiment with fun new ways of preparing whole foods, these gadgets deserve consideration.

For a new twist on everyone's favorite fried snack and comfort foods, air fryers offer a brilliantly crispy-yet-healthy method of frying up plant-based foods using little to no oil. Vegetable fries, sumptuous falafel, crispy tofu bites, and vegan chicken nuggets emerge from these sleek countertop ovens with the most irresistible crispy textures while saving you from excess oil consumption.

Meanwhile, immersion blenders let you puree hot soups and sauces directly in the pot for effortless creaminess and smooth textures. These space-saving hand blenders are perfect for whipping up quick dips, cauliflower alfredo, and other decadent sauces right in the cooking vessel. They eliminate the messy transfer to a countertop blender unit.

Then there are spiralizers – specialty tools that can transform sturdy vegetables like zucchini, sweet potatoes, and beets into long spiral noodles ready for tossing with your favorite plant-based sauces, pestos, and toppings. It's a revolutionary way to sneak more nutrient-packed produce into your everyday meals. The possibilities are endless once you unlock the spiralizing technique.

For those who simply love to explore different ways of getting creative with plant-based cooking, these functional yet fun specialty tools offer fresh new culinary frontiers to conquer. They can add exciting textural variety to the plant-based menu.

- **Curating Your Plant-Based Kitchen Hub**

  Of course, there are plenty of other handy kitchen accessories and gadgets that could be considered essential additions to the plant-based cooking space as well. The perfect arsenal will depend on your unique menu styles, food preferences, convenience needs, and culinary ambitions.

Pressure cookers, dehydrators, bread makers, ice cream machines, juicers, waffle makers, high-quality pots, pans, baking sheets, storage containers, utensils, and even a simple mortar and pestle all have worthy places of honor for different types of aspiring plant-based chefs. The key is curating the tools and technologies that will empower you to craft the wholesome, flavorful, plant-fueled dishes your culinary heart desires with efficiency and flair.

Remember, a well-stocked plant-based kitchen is one that invites you to dive in, get your hands dirty, and lose yourself in the nourishing ritual of transforming vibrant whole plant foods into artful sustenance. With the right tools at your fingertips, the process becomes creativity in action. So choose wisely, stock up, and prepare to unlock your full potential as a talented plant-based chef.

**Understanding plant-based nutrition**

For those exploring a plant-based lifestyle, one of the most common concerns tends to center around nutrition. How can someone subsisting solely on plant foods possibly meet all their nutritional needs and maintain vibrant health? The good news is that plant-based eating, when followed in a balanced and well-informed manner, can absolutely provide complete nutrition to support peak vitality.

While transitioning away from animal-based products does require some additional education and planning around optimal plant-based nutrition, the potential payoff is massive. Executed thoughtfully, a diet centered around whole plant foods contains everything your body needs to thrive while offering powerful protective benefits against chronic diseases. It all comes down to understanding which plant foods are nutrient-dense, how to achieve complementarity, and when judicious supplementation may be warranted.

- **Understanding Plant Protein Needs**

One of the most pervasive myths about vegan and vegetarian diets is that it's impossible to meet your body's protein needs from plant sources alone. However, provided you consume enough calorie-dense plant foods and eat a reasonably varied diet, getting adequate protein is very achievable on plants.

While it's true that most plant foods are lower in protein compared to animal products, they can absolutely add up over the course of a day. A lavish tofu and vegetable stir-fry, lentil soup, hummus and pita, peanut butter on whole wheat bread, edamame, nuts, quinoa, seitan, and nutritional yeast all contribute decent amounts of protein that accumulate.

The key is incorporating a variety of protein sources like beans, lentils, nuts, seeds, soy foods, whole grains, and even some vegetables over your day's meals and snacks. As long as you consume enough overall calories from nutrient-dense whole plant foods, you can easily meet the recommended daily protein target which is actually lower than most people assume.

What's more, provided you eat a few different types of plant proteins in the same day, you'll get all the essential amino acids your body requires. So while individual plant foods may be limited in certain amino acids, combining different sources like grains and legumes creates complementary proteins that form a complete amino acid profile.

- **Meeting Other Nutrient Needs**

  Moving beyond protein, most plant-based whole foods offer an impressive density of other vital vitamins, minerals, healthy fats, fiber, and protective plant compounds. Careful meal construction allows vegans and vegetarians to meet their micronutrient needs remarkably well.

  For instance, leafy greens like kale, bok choy and spinach are nutrient powerhouses packed with iron, calcium, folate, vitamin K, magnesium and more. Beans, lentils, nuts, and whole grains contribute hefty doses of fiber, iron, zinc and B vitamins. Fruits and veggies burst with vitamin C, antioxidants, and phytochemicals. Healthy fats come from olives, avocados, nuts and seeds.

By thoughtfully combining different nutrient-dense whole plant foods into your routine, you can cover your bases quite easily. The one exception is vitamin B12, which is critical for energy, red blood cell formation, and neurological function. Since B12 is primarily found in animal foods and products from animals that forage on bacteria, a vitamin supplement or B12-fortified foods like plant milks are wise for strict vegans.

- **Optimizing Your Plant-Based Plate**

To eat a balanced, nutritionally-complete plant-based diet, the key is to construct your meals using a variety of whole plant foods while aiming for an optimal balance of macronutrients and food groups. The old "food pyramid" still offers useful guidance, with some fine-tuning for plant-based applications.

At the base of your plate, emphasize generous portions of whole grains, starchy vegetables like potatoes, and fruit. This foundation should make up around 50% or more of your total caloric intake from carbohydrate sources high in fiber and nutrient density. Grains like quinoa, brown rice, barley and oats along with fruits and veggies provide essential vitamins, minerals, fiber, and protective plant compounds.

The next sizable portion of your plate should be reserved for legumes, nuts, seeds, and meat alternatives like tofu and seitan. These protein-rich stars contribute the building blocks for strong muscles along with fiber, iron, zinc and healthy fats. Aim for around 20-30% of your calories from this plant protein zone.

Finally, the remaining portion centers on health-promoting whole food fats from sources like avocados, olives, nuts, and plant oils. These satiating fats facilitate nutrient absorption while supporting hormonal balance, skin and hair health, and energy levels.

Just 20-30% of your calories should originate from fats.

With meals assembled around this blueprint, you'll hit your macro and micronutrient targets while achieving a diversity of beneficial plant compounds. Hydration, moderation, regular exercise, and quality sleep round out the recipe for whole-body thriving on a 100% plant-based diet. It's that simple - and that powerful.

- **Nutrition Mastery is a Journey**

  Of course, optimizing your plant-based nutrition isn't something that happens overnight or without some upfront education and commitment. It takes time to gain mastery at identifying nutrient-dense plant foods, combining ingredients for complementary nutrition, meal planning and prepping, discovering your favorite fortified foods and supplements, and developing a sixth sense for achieving an optimal macronutrient balance.

There will likely be some trial and error as you tweak and refine your plant-based diet until reaching that sweet spot where you feel energized, satisfied and are meeting your body's needs. Blind spots, deficiencies or excesses of certain nutrients may crop up initially until you start understanding what works best for your individual biochemistry on a vegan or vegetarian plan.

But keep an open mind, stay dedicated to the process, and don't shy away from working with qualified professionals like dieticians for guidance as you transition into plant-based living. With commitment and the right educational resources, you can absolutely thrive on a nutritionally complete, balanced, health-promoting plant-based diet for the long haul.

- **The Plant-Based Nourishment Payoff**

While developing mastery of plant-based nutrition requires effort initially, the long-term benefits more than justify the investment for those who embrace this lifestyle. Deriving your nourishment from nature's vibrant whole plant sources sets you up to experience incredible vitality and long-lasting health advantages.

Population studies consistently show that folks following balanced plant-centric diets exhibit lower risks of chronic diseases like heart disease, diabetes, obesity, and some cancers compared to the general population. Their diets tend to be lower in unhealthy saturated fats and higher in health-promoting fiber, vitamins, minerals, and phytochemicals.

When fuel from whole plant foods is properly combined using principles of plant-based nutrition mastery, you can absolutely meet all your body's needs for growth, healing, energy production and overall functioning at its absolute peak capacity. You're setting yourself up to look, feel and quite simply be your best self through the power of this conscious lifestyle.

Perhaps most importantly, shifting to a nutrient-dense plant-based diet completely transforms how you experience food. Rather than simply eating for fleeting cravings and sensory pleasure, the act of nourishing yourself is elevated to something sacred and deeply connected to living in alignment with your deepest health values.

There is profound satisfaction in knowing each forkful provides vibrant nourishment and healing potential from nature's generous bounty. That's the ultimate payoff that makes the ongoing journey of plant-based nutrition so worthwhile – food as preventive self-care, as an environmental stance, as spiritual sustenance. It's nutrition for your cells and your soul.

# Chapter 3

# Breakfast Delights

**Green Smoothie Bowl**

**Description:** A refreshing and nutritious breakfast or snack option packed with leafy greens and fruits.

**Preparation time:** 10 minutes

**Cooking time:** 0 minutes

**Number of servings:** 2

**Ingredients:**

- 2 cups fresh spinach leaves

- 1 ripe banana, sliced
- 1 green apple, cored and diced
- 1/2 cup diced cucumber
- 1/2 cup plain Greek yogurt
- 1/4 cup almond milk (or any milk of choice)
- 1 tablespoon honey or maple syrup (optional)
- Toppings: sliced kiwi, sliced strawberries, granola, chia seeds

**Directions:**

1. In a blender, combine spinach, banana, apple, cucumber, Greek yogurt, almond milk, and honey or maple syrup if using.
2. Blend until smooth and creamy, adding more almond milk if needed to reach desired consistency.

3. Pour the green smoothie into bowls.
4. Top with sliced kiwi, strawberries, granola, and chia seeds.
5. Serve immediately and enjoy!

**Nutritional info:** (per serving)

- Calories: 210
- Total Fat: 3g
- Saturated Fat: 0.5g
- Cholesterol: 5mg
- Sodium: 65mg
- Total Carbohydrates: 41g
- Dietary Fiber: 7g
- Sugars: 25g
- Protein: 10g

## Tropical Smoothie Bowl

**Description:** Transport yourself to a tropical paradise with this vibrant and delicious smoothie bowl.

**Preparation time:** 10 minutes

**Cooking time:** 0 minutes

**Number of servings:** 2

**Ingredients:**

- 1 cup frozen mango chunks
- 1 cup frozen pineapple chunks
- 1 ripe banana, sliced
- 1/2 cup coconut water or pineapple juice
- 1/4 cup plain Greek yogurt

- Toppings: sliced banana, sliced kiwi, shredded coconut, granola

**Directions:**

1. In a blender, combine frozen mango, frozen pineapple, banana, coconut water or pineapple juice, and Greek yogurt.
2. Blend until smooth and creamy, adding more liquid if necessary.
3. Pour the tropical smoothie into bowls.
4. Top with sliced banana, kiwi, shredded coconut, and granola.
5. Serve immediately and enjoy the taste of the tropics!

**Nutritional info:** (per serving)

- Calories: 280

- Total Fat: 2g
- Saturated Fat: 1g
- Cholesterol: 5mg
- Sodium: 25mg
- Total Carbohydrates: 65g
- Dietary Fiber: 8g
- Sugars: 45g
- Protein: 7g

**Peanut Butter and Jelly Smoothie**

**Description:** A nostalgic and protein-packed smoothie that tastes like your favorite childhood sandwich.

**Preparation time:** 5 minutes

**Cooking time:** 0 minutes

**Number of servings:** 1

**Ingredients:**

- 1 ripe banana
- 1/2 cup frozen strawberries
- 2 tablespoons peanut butter
- 1 cup milk (dairy or plant-based)
- 1 tablespoon honey or maple syrup (optional)
- Toppings: sliced strawberries, peanut butter drizzle, granola

**Directions:**

1. In a blender, combine banana, frozen strawberries, peanut butter, milk, and honey or maple syrup if using.

2. Blend until smooth and creamy.
3. Pour the peanut butter and jelly smoothie into a glass.
4. Top with sliced strawberries, a drizzle of peanut butter, and granola.
5. Serve immediately and enjoy this nostalgic treat!

**Nutritional info:** (per serving)

- Calories: 410
- Total Fat: 17g
- Saturated Fat: 4g
- Cholesterol: 10mg
- Sodium: 200mg
- Total Carbohydrates: 55g
- Dietary Fiber: 7g

- Sugars: 33g
- Protein: 14g

**Banana Bread Smoothie**

**Description:** Indulge in the flavors of freshly baked banana bread with this wholesome and satisfying smoothie.

**Preparation time:** 5 minutes

**Cooking time:** 0 minutes

**Number of servings:** 1

**Ingredients:**

- 1 ripe banana
- 1/4 cup rolled oats
- 1/2 cup plain Greek yogurt

- 1/2 cup milk (dairy or plant-based)
- 1/2 teaspoon ground cinnamon
- 1 tablespoon honey or maple syrup
- 1/4 teaspoon vanilla extract
- Toppings: sliced banana, chopped walnuts, sprinkle of cinnamon

**Directions:**

1. In a blender, combine banana, rolled oats, Greek yogurt, milk, cinnamon, honey or maple syrup, and vanilla extract.
2. Blend until smooth and creamy.
3. Pour the banana bread smoothie into a glass.
4. Top with sliced banana, chopped walnuts, and a sprinkle of cinnamon.

5. Serve immediately and enjoy the comforting taste of banana bread in a glass!

**Nutritional info:** (per serving)

- Calories: 350
- Total Fat: 7g
- Saturated Fat: 2g
- Cholesterol: 10mg
- Sodium: 85mg
- Total Carbohydrates: 61g
- Dietary Fiber: 6g
- Sugars: 33g
- Protein: 17g

**Mango Lassi Smoothie**

**Description:** A creamy and refreshing Indian-inspired smoothie featuring the tropical flavors of mango and yogurt.

**Preparation time:** 5 minutes

**Cooking time:** 0 minutes

**Number of servings:** 2

**Ingredients:**

- 2 ripe mangoes, peeled and diced
- 1 cup plain Greek yogurt
- 1/2 cup milk (dairy or plant-based)
- 2 tablespoons honey or maple syrup
- 1/4 teaspoon ground cardamom (optional)
- Toppings: sliced mango, chopped pistachios, pinch of ground cardamom

**Directions:**

1. In a blender, combine diced mangoes, Greek yogurt, milk, honey or maple syrup, and ground cardamom if using.
2. Blend until smooth and creamy.
3. Pour the mango lassi smoothie into glasses.
4. Top with sliced mango, chopped pistachios, and a pinch of ground cardamom.
5. Serve immediately and savor the exotic flavors of this traditional Indian beverage!

**Nutritional info:** (per serving)

- Calories: 250
- Total Fat: 3g
- Saturated Fat: 1g
- Cholesterol: 5mg

- Sodium: 50mg
- Total Carbohydrates: 52g
- Dietary Fiber: 4g
- Sugars: 46g
- Protein: 10g

**Overnight Oats with Berries**

**Description:** A delicious and convenient make-ahead breakfast featuring creamy oats soaked in milk and topped with fresh berries.

**Preparation time:** 5 minutes

Chilling time: Overnight

**Number of servings:** 2

**Ingredients:**

- 1 cup old-fashioned rolled oats
- 1 cup milk (dairy or plant-based)
- 1/4 cup Greek yogurt
- 1 tablespoon honey or maple syrup
- 1/2 teaspoon vanilla extract
- Toppings: fresh berries (strawberries, blueberries, raspberries), sliced almonds, drizzle of honey

**Directions:**

1. In a mixing bowl, combine rolled oats, milk, Greek yogurt, honey or maple syrup, and vanilla extract.
2. Stir well to combine.
3. Divide the oat mixture into two jars or bowls.
4. Cover and refrigerate overnight.

5. In the morning, top the overnight oats with fresh berries, sliced almonds, and a drizzle of honey.
6. Enjoy your nutritious and satisfying breakfast!

**Nutritional info:** (per serving)

- Calories: 250
- Total Fat: 5g
- Saturated Fat: 1g
- Cholesterol: 5mg
- Sodium: 60mg
- Total Carbohydrates: 45g
- Dietary Fiber: 6g
- Sugars: 18g
- Protein: 9g

**Chocolate Chia Pudding**

**Description:** A rich and indulgent dessert or snack made with chia seeds and cocoa powder for a chocolatey treat.

**Preparation time:** 5 minutes

Chilling time: 4 hours or overnight

**Number of servings:** 2

**Ingredients:**

- 1/4 cup chia seeds
- 1 cup milk (dairy or plant-based)
- 2 tablespoons unsweetened cocoa powder
- 2 tablespoons maple syrup or honey
- 1/2 teaspoon vanilla extract

- Toppings: sliced bananas, chopped nuts, cocoa powder

**Directions:**

1. In a mixing bowl, combine chia seeds, milk, cocoa powder, maple syrup or honey, and vanilla extract.
2. Whisk together until well combined and there are no clumps of cocoa powder.
3. Divide the mixture into two jars or bowls.
4. Cover and refrigerate for at least 4 hours or overnight, until thickened.
5. Once set, top the chocolate chia pudding with sliced bananas, chopped nuts, and a sprinkle of cocoa powder.
6. Serve chilled and enjoy the decadent chocolate flavor!

**Nutritional info:** (per serving)

- Calories: 250
- Total Fat: 12g
- Saturated Fat: 2g
- Cholesterol: 5mg
- Sodium: 60mg
- Total Carbohydrates: 32g
- Dietary Fiber: 12g
- Sugars: 15g
- Protein: 9g

**Coconut Chia Pudding**

**Description:** A creamy and tropical pudding made with chia seeds and coconut milk, perfect for a healthy dessert or snack.

**Preparation time:** 5 minutes

Chilling time: 4 hours or overnight

**Number of servings:** 2

**Ingredients:**

- 1/4 cup chia seeds
- 1 cup coconut milk (canned or carton)
- 2 tablespoons shredded coconut (unsweetened)
- 2 tablespoons maple syrup or honey
- 1/2 teaspoon vanilla extract

- Toppings: sliced mango, toasted coconut flakes, chopped pineapple

**Directions:**

1. In a mixing bowl, combine chia seeds, coconut milk, shredded coconut, maple syrup or honey, and vanilla extract.
2. Stir well to combine.
3. Divide the mixture into two jars or bowls.
4. Cover and refrigerate for at least 4 hours or overnight, until thickened.
5. Once set, top the coconut chia pudding with sliced mango, toasted coconut flakes, and chopped pineapple.
6. Serve chilled and enjoy the tropical flavors!

**Nutritional info:** (per serving)

- Calories: 300
- Total Fat: 20g
- Saturated Fat: 14g
- Cholesterol: 0mg
- Sodium: 20mg
- Total Carbohydrates: 26g
- Dietary Fiber: 10g
- Sugars: 14g
- Protein: 6g

**Carrot Cake Overnight Oats**

**Description:** All the flavors of classic carrot cake in a convenient and nutritious overnight oats recipe.

**Preparation time:** 5 minutes

Chilling time: Overnight

**Number of servings:** 2

**Ingredients:**

- 1 cup old-fashioned rolled oats
- 1 cup milk (dairy or plant-based)
- 1/4 cup grated carrot
- 2 tablespoons Greek yogurt
- 2 tablespoons maple syrup or honey
- 1/2 teaspoon ground cinnamon
- 1/4 teaspoon ground nutmeg
- Toppings: chopped walnuts, raisins, shredded coconut

**Directions:**

1. In a mixing bowl, combine rolled oats, milk, grated carrot, Greek yogurt, maple syrup or honey, cinnamon, and nutmeg.
2. Stir well to combine.
3. Divide the mixture into two jars or bowls.
4. Cover and refrigerate overnight.
5. In the morning, top the carrot cake overnight oats with chopped walnuts, raisins, and shredded coconut.
6. Serve chilled and enjoy the comforting flavors of carrot cake!

**Nutritional info:** (per serving)

- Calories: 280
- Total Fat: 5g
- Saturated Fat: 1g

- Cholesterol: 5mg
- Sodium: 60mg
- Total Carbohydrates: 50g
- Dietary Fiber: 6g
- Sugars: 18g
- Protein: 9g

**Peanut Butter Overnight Oats**

**Description:** A creamy and satisfying breakfast option featuring the irresistible flavor of peanut butter.

**Preparation time:** 5 minutes

Chilling time: Overnight

**Number of servings:** 2

**Ingredients:**

- 1 cup old-fashioned rolled oats
- 1 cup milk (dairy or plant-based)
- 2 tablespoons peanut butter
- 2 tablespoons Greek yogurt
- 2 tablespoons honey or maple syrup
- Toppings: sliced banana, chopped peanuts, drizzle of peanut butter

**Directions:**

1. In a mixing bowl, combine rolled oats, milk, peanut butter, Greek yogurt, and honey or maple syrup.
2. Stir well to combine.
3. Divide the mixture into two jars or bowls.
4. Cover and refrigerate overnight.

5. In the morning, top the peanut butter overnight oats with sliced banana, chopped peanuts, and a drizzle of peanut butter.
6. Serve chilled and enjoy the delicious combination of oats and peanut butter!

**Nutritional info:** (per serving)

- Calories: 350
- Total Fat: 14g
- Saturated Fat: 3g
- Cholesterol: 5mg
- Sodium: 65mg
- Total Carbohydrates: 47g
- Dietary Fiber: 5g
- Sugars: 17g
- Protein: 12g

## Tofu Scramble with Veggies

**Description:** A flavorful and protein-packed vegan breakfast option featuring tofu scrambled with colorful vegetables.

**Preparation time:** 10 minutes

**Cooking time:** 10 minutes

**Number of servings:** 2

**Ingredients:**

- 1 block firm tofu, drained and crumbled
- 1 tablespoon olive oil
- 1/2 onion, diced
- 1 bell pepper, diced
- 1 cup spinach leaves

- 1/2 teaspoon turmeric powder
- Salt and pepper to taste
- Optional toppings: sliced avocado, chopped fresh herbs

**Directions:**

1. Heat olive oil in a skillet over medium heat.
2. Add diced onion and bell pepper to the skillet. Sauté until softened, about 3-4 minutes.
3. Add crumbled tofu to the skillet, along with turmeric powder, salt, and pepper. Cook for another 5-6 minutes, stirring occasionally, until tofu is heated through and slightly golden.
4. Add spinach leaves to the skillet and cook until wilted.

5. Remove from heat and serve the tofu scramble with optional toppings such as sliced avocado and chopped fresh herbs.
6. Enjoy this delicious and nutritious vegan breakfast!

**Nutritional info:** (per serving)

- Calories: 180
- Total Fat: 11g
- Saturated Fat: 1.5g
- Cholesterol: 0mg
- Sodium: 180mg
- Total Carbohydrates: 8g
- Dietary Fiber: 3g
- Sugars: 3g
- Protein: 14g

**Chickpea Omelet**

**Description:** A vegan twist on the classic omelet, made with chickpea flour and filled with your favorite veggies.

**Preparation time:** 10 minutes

**Cooking time:** 10 minutes

**Number of servings:** 1

**Ingredients:**

- 1/2 cup chickpea flour
- 1/2 cup water
- 1/4 teaspoon baking powder
- Salt and pepper to taste

- 1/4 cup diced vegetables (such as bell peppers, onions, tomatoes)
- 1 tablespoon chopped fresh herbs (such as parsley or cilantro)
- 1 tablespoon olive oil

**Directions:**

1. In a mixing bowl, whisk together chickpea flour, water, baking powder, salt, and pepper until smooth.
2. Stir in diced vegetables and chopped fresh herbs.
3. Heat olive oil in a non-stick skillet over medium heat.
4. Pour the chickpea batter into the skillet and spread it evenly.

5. Cook for 3-4 minutes, or until the edges start to set and bubbles form on the surface.
6. Carefully flip the omelet and cook for another 2-3 minutes, or until cooked through.
7. Fold the omelet in half and transfer to a plate.
8. Serve hot and enjoy this plant-based alternative to traditional omelets!

**Nutritional info:** (per serving)

- Calories: 280
- Total Fat: 14g
- Saturated Fat: 2g
- Cholesterol: 0mg
- Sodium: 320mg
- Total Carbohydrates: 30g
- Dietary Fiber: 7g

- Sugars: 4g
- Protein: 12g

### Tofu Frittata with Spinach and Mushrooms

**Description:** A savory and satisfying vegan frittata made with tofu, spinach, and mushrooms.

**Preparation time:** 15 minutes

**Cooking time:** 25 minutes

**Number of servings:** 4

**Ingredients:**

- 1 block firm tofu, drained and crumbled
- 1 tablespoon olive oil

- 1/2 onion, diced
- 1 cup sliced mushrooms
- 2 cups fresh spinach leaves
- 1/4 cup nutritional yeast
- 1/2 teaspoon garlic powder
- Salt and pepper to taste
- Optional toppings: sliced cherry tomatoes, chopped fresh herbs

**Directions:**

1. Preheat the oven to 375°F (190°C).
2. Heat olive oil in an oven-safe skillet over medium heat.
3. Add diced onion to the skillet and sauté until softened, about 3-4 minutes.

4. Add sliced mushrooms to the skillet and cook until they release their moisture and start to brown.
5. Add crumbled tofu to the skillet, along with nutritional yeast, garlic powder, salt, and pepper. Stir well to combine.
6. Stir in fresh spinach leaves and cook until wilted.
7. Smooth the top of the tofu mixture with a spatula and transfer the skillet to the preheated oven.
8. Bake for 20-25 minutes, or until the frittata is set and lightly golden on top.
9. Remove from the oven and let it cool slightly before slicing.

10. Serve the tofu frittata with optional toppings such as sliced cherry tomatoes and chopped fresh herbs.
11. Enjoy this hearty and nutritious vegan dish for breakfast, brunch, or any meal of the day!

**Nutritional info:** (per serving)

- Calories: 160
- Total Fat: 9g
- Saturated Fat: 1g
- Cholesterol: 0mg
- Sodium: 140mg
- Total Carbohydrates: 8g
- Dietary Fiber: 3g
- Sugars: 2g
- Protein: 14g

**Vegan Omelet with Cashew Cheese**

**Description:** A dairy-free omelet filled with creamy cashew cheese and your favorite veggies for a satisfying breakfast or brunch.

**Preparation time:** 15 minutes

**Cooking time:** 10 minutes

**Number of servings:** 1

**Ingredients:**

- 1/2 cup chickpea flour
- 1/2 cup water
- 1/4 teaspoon baking powder
- Salt and pepper to taste
- 2 tablespoons cashew cheese

- 1/4 cup diced vegetables (such as bell peppers, onions, spinach)
- 1 tablespoon chopped fresh herbs (such as parsley or chives)
- 1 tablespoon olive oil

**Directions:**

1. In a mixing bowl, whisk together chickpea flour, water, baking powder, salt, and pepper until smooth.
2. Stir in diced vegetables and chopped fresh herbs.
3. Heat olive oil in a non-stick skillet over medium heat.
4. Pour half of the chickpea batter into the skillet and spread it evenly.

5. Cook for 3-4 minutes, or until the edges start to set and bubbles form on the surface.
6. Carefully spread cashew cheese on one half of the omelet.
7. Fold the other half of the omelet over the cheese and cook for another 2-3 minutes, or until cooked through.
8. Repeat with the remaining batter to make another omelet.
9. Serve hot and enjoy this delicious vegan alternative to traditional omelets!

**Nutritional info:** (per serving)

- Calories: 320
- Total Fat: 16g
- Saturated Fat: 3g

- Cholesterol: 0mg
- Sodium: 320mg
- Total Carbohydrates: 30g
- Dietary Fiber: 7g
- Sugars: 4g
- Protein: 14g

**Tempeh Bacon and Tofu Scramble**

**Description:** A savory and satisfying vegan breakfast featuring tempeh bacon and tofu scrambled with flavorful seasonings.

**Preparation time:** 15 minutes

**Cooking time:** 15 minutes

**Number of servings:** 2

**Ingredients:**

- 1 block firm tofu, drained and crumbled
- 1 tablespoon olive oil
- 4 slices tempeh bacon
- 1/2 onion, diced
- 1 bell pepper, diced
- 1/2 teaspoon garlic powder
- 1/2 teaspoon smoked paprika
- Salt and pepper to taste
- Optional toppings: sliced avocado, chopped fresh herbs

**Directions:**

1. Heat olive oil in a skillet over medium heat.

2. Add tempeh bacon slices to the skillet and cook until crispy on both sides. Remove from the skillet and set aside.
3. In the same skillet, add diced onion and bell pepper. Sauté until softened, about 3-4 minutes.
4. Add crumbled tofu to the skillet, along with garlic powder, smoked paprika, salt, and pepper. Cook for another 5-6 minutes, stirring occasionally, until tofu is heated through and slightly golden.
5. Crumble the cooked tempeh bacon into the tofu scramble and stir to combine.
6. Remove from heat and serve the tempeh bacon and tofu scramble with optional toppings such as sliced avocado and chopped fresh herbs.

7. Enjoy this hearty and flavorful vegan breakfast!

**Nutritional info:** (per serving)

- Calories: 280
- Total Fat: 16g
- Saturated Fat: 3g
- Cholesterol: 0mg
- Sodium: 260mg
- Total Carbohydrates: 12g
- Dietary Fiber: 5g
- Sugars: 3g
- Protein: 20g

**Vegan Banana Pancakes**

**Description:** Fluffy and delicious pancakes made without eggs or dairy, featuring ripe bananas for natural sweetness.

**Preparation time:** 10 minutes

**Cooking time:** 10 minutes

**Number of servings:** 2-3

**Ingredients:**

- 1 ripe banana, mashed
- 1 cup all-purpose flour
- 1 tablespoon sugar
- 1 tablespoon baking powder
- 1/4 teaspoon salt
- 1 cup non-dairy milk (such as almond milk or oat milk)

- 1 teaspoon vanilla extract
- Optional toppings: sliced bananas, maple syrup, chopped nuts

**Directions:**

1. In a mixing bowl, combine mashed banana, flour, sugar, baking powder, and salt.
2. Stir in non-dairy milk and vanilla extract until smooth.
3. Heat a non-stick skillet or griddle over medium heat and lightly grease with oil or cooking spray.
4. Pour 1/4 cup of batter onto the skillet for each pancake.
5. Cook for 2-3 minutes, or until bubbles form on the surface of the pancake.

6. Flip and cook for another 2-3 minutes, or until golden brown.
7. Repeat with the remaining batter.
8. Serve the vegan banana pancakes warm with your favorite toppings such as sliced bananas, maple syrup, and chopped nuts.
9. Enjoy this wholesome and satisfying breakfast treat!

**Nutritional info:** (per serving, without toppings)

- Calories: 220
- Total Fat: 2g
- Saturated Fat: 0g
- Cholesterol: 0mg
- Sodium: 480mg

- Total Carbohydrates: 46g
- Dietary Fiber: 2g
- Sugars: 9g
- Protein: 5g

**Whole Wheat Vegan Waffles**

**Description:** Nutritious and wholesome waffles made with whole wheat flour and plant-based ingredients.

**Preparation time:** 10 minutes

**Cooking time:** 10 minutes

**Number of servings:** 2-3

**Ingredients:**

- 1 1/2 cups whole wheat flour

- 2 tablespoons sugar
- 1 tablespoon baking powder
- 1/4 teaspoon salt
- 1 1/4 cups non-dairy milk (such as soy milk or coconut milk)
- 1/4 cup unsweetened applesauce
- 2 tablespoons melted coconut oil or vegetable oil
- 1 teaspoon vanilla extract

**Directions:**

1. Preheat your waffle iron according to manufacturer's instructions.
2. In a large mixing bowl, whisk together whole wheat flour, sugar, baking powder, and salt.

3. In a separate bowl, combine non-dairy milk, applesauce, melted coconut oil or vegetable oil, and vanilla extract.
4. Pour the wet ingredients into the dry ingredients and stir until just combined. Do not overmix.
5. Lightly grease the waffle iron with oil or cooking spray.
6. Pour enough batter onto the hot waffle iron to cover the grids.
7. Close the waffle iron and cook according to manufacturer's instructions, until golden brown and crispy.
8. Carefully remove the waffles from the iron and repeat with the remaining batter.

9. Serve the whole wheat vegan waffles warm with your favorite toppings such as fresh fruit, maple syrup, or nut butter.
10. Enjoy this nutritious and delicious breakfast!

    **Nutritional info:** (per serving, without toppings)

- Calories: 300
- Total Fat: 9g
- Saturated Fat: 6g
- Cholesterol: 0mg
- Sodium: 490mg
- Total Carbohydrates: 47g
- Dietary Fiber: 5g
- Sugars: 8g
- Protein: 8g

**Blueberry Buckwheat Pancakes**

**Description:** Hearty and wholesome pancakes made with nutrient-rich buckwheat flour and bursting with juicy blueberries.

**Preparation time:** 10 minutes

**Cooking time:** 10 minutes

**Number of servings:** 2-3

**Ingredients:**

- 1 cup buckwheat flour
- 1 tablespoon sugar
- 1 tablespoon baking powder
- 1/4 teaspoon salt

- 1 cup non-dairy milk (such as almond milk or soy milk)
- 1 tablespoon melted coconut oil or vegetable oil
- 1 teaspoon vanilla extract
- 1/2 cup fresh or frozen blueberries

**Directions:**

1. In a mixing bowl, whisk together buckwheat flour, sugar, baking powder, and salt.
2. In a separate bowl, combine non-dairy milk, melted coconut oil or vegetable oil, and vanilla extract.
3. Pour the wet ingredients into the dry ingredients and stir until just combined.
4. Gently fold in the blueberries.

5. Heat a non-stick skillet or griddle over medium heat and lightly grease with oil or cooking spray.
6. Pour 1/4 cup of batter onto the skillet for each pancake.
7. Cook for 2-3 minutes, or until bubbles form on the surface of the pancake.
8. Flip and cook for another 2-3 minutes, or until golden brown.
9. Repeat with the remaining batter.
10. Serve the blueberry buckwheat pancakes warm with maple syrup or your favorite toppings.
11. Enjoy these nutritious and flavorful pancakes for breakfast or brunch!

**Nutritional info:** (per serving, without toppings)

- Calories: 240
- Total Fat: 8g
- Saturated Fat: 4g
- Cholesterol: 0mg
- Sodium: 490mg
- Total Carbohydrates: 35g
- Dietary Fiber: 4g
- Sugars: 6g
- Protein: 6g

**French Toast with Coconut Whipped Cream**

**Description:** Classic French toast made with thick slices of bread soaked in a rich custard mixture, served with decadent coconut whipped cream.

**Preparation time:** 15 minutes

**Cooking time:** 10 minutes

**Number of servings:** 2-3

**Ingredients:**

For the French toast:

- 4 slices thick bread (such as challah or brioche)
- 1 cup non-dairy milk (such as coconut milk or almond milk)
- 2 tablespoons chickpea flour or cornstarch
- 1 tablespoon maple syrup
- 1 teaspoon vanilla extract
- 1/2 teaspoon ground cinnamon

- Pinch of salt
- Coconut oil or vegan butter for cooking

For the coconut whipped cream:

- 1 can (13.5 oz) full-fat coconut milk, refrigerated overnight
- 2 tablespoons powdered sugar
- 1/2 teaspoon vanilla extract

Optional toppings:

- Maple syrup
- Fresh berries
- Toasted coconut flakes

**Directions:**

1. Prepare the coconut whipped cream: Remove the can of coconut milk from the refrigerator

without shaking it. Open the can and scoop out the solid coconut cream that has risen to the top, leaving behind the coconut water at the bottom.

2. Place the solid coconut cream in a mixing bowl and add powdered sugar and vanilla extract.
3. Using a hand mixer or stand mixer, whip the coconut cream until light and fluffy. Refrigerate until ready to use.
4. Prepare the French toast: In a shallow dish, whisk together non-dairy milk, chickpea flour or cornstarch, maple syrup, vanilla extract, cinnamon, and salt until well combined.
5. Heat coconut oil or vegan butter in a large skillet over medium heat.

6. Dip each slice of bread into the custard mixture, allowing it to soak for a few seconds on each side.
7. Place the soaked bread slices in the skillet and cook for 2-3 minutes on each side, or until golden brown and crispy.
8. Serve the French toast warm with a dollop of coconut whipped cream and your favorite toppings such as maple syrup, fresh berries, or toasted coconut flakes.
9. Enjoy this indulgent and delicious breakfast or brunch treat!

**Nutritional info:** (per serving, without toppings)

French Toast:

- Calories: 240
- Total Fat: 6g
- Saturated Fat: 3g
- Cholesterol: 0mg
- Sodium: 280mg
- Total Carbohydrates: 40g
- Dietary Fiber: 2g
- Sugars: 8g
- Protein: 6g

Coconut Whipped Cream:

- Calories: 80
- Total Fat: 8g
- Saturated Fat: 7g
- Cholesterol: 0mg
- Sodium: 5mg

- Total Carbohydrates: 2g
- Dietary Fiber: 0g
- Sugars: 1g
- Protein: 0g

**Sweet Potato Pancakes**

**Description:** Flavorful and nutritious pancakes made with mashed sweet potatoes and warm spices.

**Preparation time:** 15 minutes

**Cooking time:** 10 minutes

**Number of servings:** 2-3

**Ingredients:**

- 1 cup mashed sweet potatoes (from about 2 medium sweet potatoes)
- 1 cup all-purpose flour
- 1 tablespoon sugar
- 1 tablespoon baking powder
- 1/2 teaspoon ground cinnamon
- 1/4 teaspoon ground nutmeg
- 1/4 teaspoon salt
- 1 cup non-dairy milk (such as almond milk or coconut milk)
- 1 tablespoon melted coconut oil or vegetable oil
- 1 teaspoon vanilla extract

**Directions:**

1. In a mixing bowl, whisk together mashed sweet potatoes, flour, sugar, baking powder, cinnamon, nutmeg, and salt until well combined.
2. In a separate bowl, combine non-dairy milk, melted coconut oil or vegetable oil, and vanilla extract.
3. Pour the wet ingredients into the dry ingredients and stir until just combined.
4. Heat a non-stick skillet or griddle over medium heat and lightly grease with oil or cooking spray.
5. Pour 1/4 cup of batter onto the skillet for each pancake.
6. Cook for 2-3 minutes, or until bubbles form on the surface of the pancake.

7. Flip and cook for another 2-3 minutes, or until golden brown.
8. Repeat with the remaining batter.
9. Serve the sweet potato pancakes warm with your favorite toppings such as maple syrup, chopped nuts, or a sprinkle of cinnamon.
10. Enjoy these flavorful and nutritious pancakes for a delicious breakfast or brunch!

**Nutritional info:** (per serving, without toppings)

- Calories: 240
- Total Fat: 6g
- Saturated Fat: 4g
- Cholesterol: 0mg
- Sodium: 490mg

- Total Carbohydrates: 40g
- Dietary Fiber: 4g
- Sugars: 8g
- Protein: 5g

**Cornbread Waffles**

**Description:** A delightful twist on traditional waffles, these cornbread waffles are crispy on the outside and tender on the inside, with a delicious cornmeal flavor.

**Preparation time:** 10 minutes

**Cooking time:** 10 minutes

**Number of servings:** 4

**Ingredients:**

- 1 cup all-purpose flour
- 1 cup cornmeal
- 2 tablespoons sugar
- 1 tablespoon baking powder
- 1/2 teaspoon salt
- 1 1/4 cups non-dairy milk (such as almond milk or soy milk)
- 1/4 cup melted vegan butter or coconut oil
- 2 tablespoons maple syrup
- Optional toppings: vegan butter, maple syrup, fresh fruit

**Directions:**

1. Preheat your waffle iron according to manufacturer's instructions.

2. In a large mixing bowl, whisk together flour, cornmeal, sugar, baking powder, and salt.
3. In a separate bowl, combine non-dairy milk, melted vegan butter or coconut oil, and maple syrup.
4. Pour the wet ingredients into the dry ingredients and stir until just combined. Do not overmix.
5. Lightly grease the waffle iron with oil or cooking spray.
6. Pour enough batter onto the hot waffle iron to cover the grids.
7. Close the waffle iron and cook according to manufacturer's instructions, until golden brown and crispy.

8. Carefully remove the cornbread waffles from the iron and repeat with the remaining batter.
9. Serve the waffles warm with your favorite toppings such as vegan butter, maple syrup, or fresh fruit.
10. Enjoy these savory-sweet waffles for breakfast or brunch!

    **Nutritional info:** (per serving, without toppings)

- Calories: 320
- Total Fat: 12g
- Saturated Fat: 6g
- Cholesterol: 0mg
- Sodium: 500mg
- Total Carbohydrates: 48g

- Dietary Fiber: 3g
- Sugars: 8g
- Protein: 5g

**Pumpkin Pancakes**

**Description:** Fluffy and flavorful pancakes made with pumpkin puree and warm spices, perfect for a cozy fall breakfast.

**Preparation time:** 10 minutes

**Cooking time:** 10 minutes

**Number of servings:** 4

**Ingredients:**

- 1 1/2 cups all-purpose flour
- 2 tablespoons brown sugar

- 1 tablespoon baking powder
- 1/2 teaspoon ground cinnamon
- 1/4 teaspoon ground nutmeg
- 1/4 teaspoon ground ginger
- Pinch of ground cloves
- Pinch of salt
- 1 cup non-dairy milk (such as almond milk or oat milk)
- 1/2 cup pumpkin puree
- 2 tablespoons melted vegan butter or coconut oil
- 1 teaspoon vanilla extract

Optional toppings:

- Maple syrup
- Chopped pecans

- Vegan whipped cream

**Directions:**

1. In a large mixing bowl, whisk together flour, brown sugar, baking powder, cinnamon, nutmeg, ginger, cloves, and salt.
2. In a separate bowl, combine non-dairy milk, pumpkin puree, melted vegan butter or coconut oil, and vanilla extract.
3. Pour the wet ingredients into the dry ingredients and stir until just combined. Do not overmix.
4. Heat a non-stick skillet or griddle over medium heat and lightly grease with oil or cooking spray.
5. Pour 1/4 cup of batter onto the skillet for each pancake.

6. Cook for 2-3 minutes, or until bubbles form on the surface of the pancake.
7. Flip and cook for another 2-3 minutes, or until golden brown.
8. Repeat with the remaining batter.
9. Serve the pumpkin pancakes warm with your favorite toppings such as maple syrup, chopped pecans, or vegan whipped cream.
10. Enjoy these cozy and flavorful pancakes for a delicious fall breakfast!

**Nutritional info:** (per serving, without toppings)

- Calories: 250
- Total Fat: 6g
- Saturated Fat: 3g

- Cholesterol: 0mg
- Sodium: 480mg
- Total Carbohydrates: 42g
- Dietary Fiber: 3g
- Sugars: 9g
- Protein: 5g

**Cinnamon Roll Pancakes**

**Description:** Indulgent pancakes with swirls of cinnamon sugar, topped with a creamy glaze for a delicious breakfast reminiscent of cinnamon rolls.

**Preparation time:** 15 minutes

**Cooking time:** 10 minutes

**Number of servings:** 4

**Ingredients:**

For the cinnamon swirl:

- 1/4 cup vegan butter, melted
- 1/4 cup brown sugar
- 1 tablespoon ground cinnamon

For the pancake batter:

- 1 1/2 cups all-purpose flour
- 2 tablespoons sugar
- 1 tablespoon baking powder
- 1/2 teaspoon salt
- 1 cup non-dairy milk (such as almond milk or soy milk)

- 2 tablespoons melted vegan butter or coconut oil
- 1 teaspoon vanilla extract

For the glaze:

- 1/2 cup powdered sugar
- 1-2 tablespoons non-dairy milk
- 1/2 teaspoon vanilla extract

**Directions:**

1. Prepare the cinnamon swirl: In a small bowl, mix together melted vegan butter, brown sugar, and ground cinnamon until well combined. Transfer the mixture to a piping bag or plastic squeeze bottle.

2. Prepare the pancake batter: In a large mixing bowl, whisk together flour, sugar, baking powder, and salt.
3. In a separate bowl, combine non-dairy milk, melted vegan butter or coconut oil, and vanilla extract.
4. Pour the wet ingredients into the dry ingredients and stir until just combined. Do not overmix.
5. Heat a non-stick skillet or griddle over medium heat and lightly grease with oil or cooking spray.
6. Pour a small amount of pancake batter onto the skillet to form a small pancake.
7. Pipe the cinnamon swirl mixture onto the pancake in a spiral pattern.

8. Cook for 2-3 minutes, or until bubbles form on the surface of the pancake.
9. Flip and cook for another 2-3 minutes, or until golden brown.
10. Repeat with the remaining batter and cinnamon swirl mixture.
11. Prepare the glaze: In a small bowl, whisk together powdered sugar, non-dairy milk, and vanilla extract until smooth.
12. Drizzle the glaze over the cooked pancakes.
13. Serve the cinnamon roll pancakes warm and enjoy this indulgent breakfast treat!

**Nutritional info:** (per serving, without toppings)

- Calories: 350
- Total Fat: 10g

- Saturated Fat: 5g
- Cholesterol: 0mg
- Sodium: 490mg
- Total Carbohydrates: 60g
- Dietary Fiber: 2g
- Sugars: 22g
- Protein: 5g

**Baked Vegan French Toast**

**Description:** A simple and delicious make-ahead breakfast featuring thick slices of bread soaked in a sweet custard mixture and baked until golden brown.

**Preparation time:** 15 minutes

Baking time: 25 minutes

**Number of servings:** 4

**Ingredients:**

- 8 slices thick bread (such as French bread or brioche)
- 1 cup non-dairy milk (such as almond milk or coconut milk)
- 1/4 cup maple syrup
- 1 tablespoon melted vegan butter or coconut oil
- 1 teaspoon vanilla extract
- 1/2 teaspoon ground cinnamon
- Pinch of salt

Optional toppings:

- Fresh berries
- Maple syrup
- Vegan whipped cream

**Directions:**

1. Preheat your oven to 375°F (190°C). Lightly grease a baking dish with vegan butter or coconut oil.
2. Arrange the slices of bread in the prepared baking dish, overlapping slightly if necessary.
3. In a mixing bowl, whisk together non-dairy milk, maple syrup, melted vegan butter or coconut oil, vanilla extract, cinnamon, and salt.
4. Pour the custard mixture over the bread slices, making sure to coat each slice evenly.

5. Let the bread soak in the custard mixture for about 10 minutes, pressing down gently to ensure absorption.
6. Bake in the preheated oven for 25-30 minutes, or until the French toast is golden brown and set.
7. Remove from the oven and let it cool slightly before serving.
8. Serve the baked vegan French toast warm with your favorite toppings such as fresh berries, maple syrup, or vegan whipped cream.
9. Enjoy this easy and delicious breakfast that can be prepared in advance!

**Nutritional info:** (per serving, without toppings)

- Calories: 280

- Total Fat: 7g
- Saturated Fat: 4g
- Cholesterol: 0mg
- Sodium: 480mg
- Total Carbohydrates: 47g
- Dietary Fiber: 2g
- Sugars: 15g
- Protein: 7g

**Lemon Ricotta Pancakes (with vegan ricotta)**

**Description:** Light and fluffy pancakes infused with bright lemon flavor and creamy vegan ricotta cheese.

**Preparation time:** 15 minutes

**Cooking time:** 10 minutes

**Number of servings:** 4

**Ingredients:**

- 1 1/2 cups all-purpose flour
- 2 tablespoons sugar
- 1 tablespoon baking powder
- 1/2 teaspoon salt
- Zest of 1 lemon
- 1 cup non-dairy milk (such as almond milk or soy milk)
- 1/2 cup vegan ricotta cheese
- 2 tablespoons melted vegan butter or coconut oil
- 1 tablespoon lemon juice

- 1 teaspoon vanilla extract

Optional toppings:

- Fresh berries
- Maple syrup
- Lemon zest

**Directions:**

1. In a large mixing bowl, whisk together flour, sugar, baking powder, salt, and lemon zest.
2. In a separate bowl, combine non-dairy milk, vegan ricotta cheese, melted vegan butter or coconut oil, lemon juice, and vanilla extract.
3. Pour the wet ingredients into the dry ingredients and stir until just combined. Do not overmix.

4. Heat a non-stick skillet or griddle over medium heat and lightly grease with oil or cooking spray.
5. Pour 1/4 cup of batter onto the skillet for each pancake.
6. Cook for 2-3 minutes, or until bubbles form on the surface of the pancake.
7. Flip and cook for another 2-3 minutes, or until golden brown.
8. Repeat with the remaining batter.
9. Serve the lemon ricotta pancakes warm with your favorite toppings such as fresh berries, maple syrup, or lemon zest.
10. Enjoy these light and flavorful pancakes for a delightful breakfast or brunch!

**Nutritional info:** (per serving, without toppings)

- Calories: 280
- Total Fat: 9g
- Saturated Fat: 5g
- Cholesterol: 0mg
- Sodium: 480mg
- Total Carbohydrates: 42g
- Dietary Fiber: 2g
- Sugars: 8g
- Protein: 7g

# Chapter 4

# Salads and Soups

## Rainbow Veggie Salad

**Description:** A vibrant and nutritious salad featuring a colorful array of fresh vegetables.

**Preparation time:** 15 minutes

**Cooking time:** 0 minutes

**Number of servings:** 4

**Ingredients:**

- 2 cups mixed salad greens
- 1 bell pepper, thinly sliced

- 1 cup cherry tomatoes, halved
- 1/2 cucumber, thinly sliced
- 1/4 red onion, thinly sliced
- 1/2 cup shredded carrots
- 1/4 cup sliced black olives
- 1/4 cup crumbled feta cheese (optional)
- 1/4 cup balsamic vinaigrette

**Directions:**

1. In a large salad bowl, combine the mixed greens, bell pepper, cherry tomatoes, cucumber, red onion, shredded carrots, and black olives.
2. Toss the salad ingredients together until well mixed.

3. Drizzle the balsamic vinaigrette over the salad and toss again to coat evenly.
4. If desired, sprinkle crumbled feta cheese over the top.
5. Serve immediately and enjoy!

**Nutritional info:**

- Calories per serving: 120
- Total fat: 7g
- Cholesterol: 5mg
- Sodium: 200mg
- Total carbohydrates: 14g
- Dietary fiber: 3g
- Sugars: 8g
- Protein: 3g

## Kale and Quinoa Salad with Lemon Vinaigrette

**Description:** A hearty and nutritious salad featuring kale, quinoa, and a zesty lemon vinaigrette.

**Preparation time:** 20 minutes

**Cooking time:** 15 minutes

**Number of servings:** 4

**Ingredients:**

- 1 cup quinoa, rinsed
- 2 cups water or vegetable broth
- 4 cups chopped kale leaves
- 1/4 cup dried cranberries
- 1/4 cup chopped almonds

- 1/4 cup crumbled feta cheese (optional)

Lemon Vinaigrette:

- 1/4 cup olive oil
- 2 tablespoons fresh lemon juice
- 1 teaspoon honey or maple syrup
- 1 teaspoon Dijon mustard
- Salt and pepper to taste

**Directions:**

1. In a medium saucepan, bring the water or vegetable broth to a boil. Add the quinoa, reduce heat to low, cover, and simmer for 15 minutes or until all the liquid is absorbed. Remove from heat and let it cool.

2. In a large salad bowl, combine the cooked quinoa, chopped kale, dried cranberries, chopped almonds, and crumbled feta cheese.
3. In a small bowl, whisk together the olive oil, lemon juice, honey or maple syrup, Dijon mustard, salt, and pepper to make the lemon vinaigrette.
4. Pour the lemon vinaigrette over the salad and toss until everything is well coated.
5. Serve immediately, or refrigerate for later. Enjoy!

**Nutritional info:**

- Calories per serving: 320
- Total fat: 16g
- Cholesterol: 5mg

- Sodium: 150mg
- Total carbohydrates: 38g
- Dietary fiber: 6g
- Sugars: 8g
- Protein: 9g

**Mediterranean Chickpea Salad**

**Description:** A refreshing salad packed with Mediterranean flavors, featuring chickpeas, cucumbers, tomatoes, and feta cheese.

**Preparation time:** 15 minutes

**Cooking time:** 0 minutes

**Number of servings:** 4

**Ingredients:**

- 2 cans (15 ounces each) chickpeas, drained and rinsed
- 1 cucumber, diced
- 1 cup cherry tomatoes, halved
- 1/4 cup diced red onion
- 1/4 cup chopped fresh parsley
- 1/4 cup crumbled feta cheese
- 2 tablespoons extra virgin olive oil
- 2 tablespoons lemon juice
- 1 teaspoon dried oregano
- Salt and pepper to taste

**Directions:**

1. In a large salad bowl, combine the chickpeas, diced cucumber, cherry tomatoes, red onion, chopped parsley, and crumbled feta cheese.

2. In a small bowl, whisk together the extra virgin olive oil, lemon juice, dried oregano, salt, and pepper to make the dressing.
3. Pour the dressing over the salad and toss until everything is evenly coated.
4. Serve immediately or refrigerate for later. Enjoy!

**Nutritional info:**

- Calories per serving: 280
- Total fat: 12g
- Cholesterol: 10mg
- Sodium: 420mg
- Total carbohydrates: 35g
- Dietary fiber: 9g
- Sugars: 7g

- Protein: 11g

**Thai Mango Salad**

**Description:** A refreshing and tangy salad featuring ripe mangoes, crunchy vegetables, and a zesty Thai-inspired dressing.

**Preparation time:** 20 minutes

**Cooking time:** 0 minutes

**Number of servings:** 4

**Ingredients:**

- 2 ripe mangoes, peeled and diced
- 1 red bell pepper, thinly sliced
- 1/2 cup shredded carrots
- 1/4 cup chopped fresh cilantro

- 1/4 cup chopped peanuts
- 2 tablespoons lime juice
- 1 tablespoon fish sauce (or soy sauce for a vegetarian version)
- 1 tablespoon honey or maple syrup
- 1 teaspoon minced garlic
- 1 teaspoon grated ginger
- 1 red chili, thinly sliced (optional)

**Directions:**

1. In a large salad bowl, combine the diced mangoes, sliced red bell pepper, shredded carrots, chopped cilantro, and chopped peanuts.
2. In a small bowl, whisk together the lime juice, fish sauce (or soy sauce), honey or maple syrup,

minced garlic, and grated ginger to make the dressing.

3. Pour the dressing over the salad and toss until everything is well coated.
4. If desired, garnish with thinly sliced red chili for an extra kick.
5. Serve immediately and enjoy the refreshing flavors!

**Nutritional info:**

- Calories per serving: 200
- Total fat: 8g
- Cholesterol: 0mg
- Sodium: 300mg
- Total carbohydrates: 32g
- Dietary fiber: 5g

- Sugars: 24g
- Protein: 4g

**Roasted Beet and Arugula Salad**

**Description:** A sophisticated salad combining earthy roasted beets with peppery arugula and a tangy balsamic dressing.

**Preparation time:** 15 minutes

**Cooking time:** 45 minutes

**Number of servings:** 4

**Ingredients:**

- 4 medium-sized beets, peeled and diced
- 4 cups baby arugula
- 1/4 cup crumbled goat cheese

- 1/4 cup chopped walnuts
- 2 tablespoons balsamic vinegar
- 2 tablespoons extra virgin olive oil
- 1 teaspoon honey or maple syrup
- Salt and pepper to taste

**Directions:**

1. Preheat the oven to 400°F (200°C). Place the diced beets on a baking sheet, drizzle with olive oil, and season with salt and pepper. Roast in the oven for 40-45 minutes, or until tender.
2. In a large salad bowl, combine the roasted beets, baby arugula, crumbled goat cheese, and chopped walnuts.

3. In a small bowl, whisk together the balsamic vinegar, extra virgin olive oil, honey or maple syrup, salt, and pepper to make the dressing.
4. Pour the dressing over the salad and toss until everything is well coated.
5. Serve immediately and enjoy the delightful combination of flavors and textures!

**Nutritional info:**

- Calories per serving: 220
- Total fat: 14g
- Cholesterol: 5mg
- Sodium: 200mg
- Total carbohydrates: 20g
- Dietary fiber: 5g
- Sugars: 14g

- Protein: 6g

**Lentil and Sweet Potato Soup**

**Description:** A hearty and nutritious soup featuring lentils, sweet potatoes, and a blend of savory spices.

**Preparation time:** 15 minutes

**Cooking time:** 40 minutes

**Number of servings:** 6

**Ingredients:**

- 1 tablespoon olive oil
- 1 onion, diced
- 2 cloves garlic, minced
- 2 carrots, diced

- 2 celery stalks, diced
- 1 sweet potato, peeled and diced
- 1 cup dried green or brown lentils, rinsed
- 6 cups vegetable broth
- 1 teaspoon ground cumin
- 1 teaspoon ground coriander
- 1/2 teaspoon smoked paprika
- Salt and pepper to taste
- Fresh cilantro or parsley for garnish (optional)

**Directions:**

1. In a large pot, heat the olive oil over medium heat. Add the diced onion and cook until softened, about 5 minutes.

2. Add the minced garlic, diced carrots, and diced celery to the pot. Cook for another 5 minutes, stirring occasionally.
3. Add the diced sweet potato, rinsed lentils, vegetable broth, ground cumin, ground coriander, smoked paprika, salt, and pepper to the pot. Stir to combine.
4. Bring the soup to a boil, then reduce the heat to low and simmer for 30 minutes, or until the lentils and sweet potatoes are tender.
5. Taste and adjust seasoning if needed. Serve hot, garnished with fresh cilantro or parsley if desired. Enjoy!

**Nutritional info:**

- Calories per serving: 250
- Total fat: 3g

- Cholesterol: 0mg
- Sodium: 700mg
- Total carbohydrates: 46g
- Dietary fiber: 14g
- Sugars: 7g
- Protein: 13g

**Creamy Vegan Broccoli Soup**

**Description:** A silky smooth and creamy soup made with tender broccoli florets and coconut milk.

**Preparation time:** 10 minutes

**Cooking time:** 25 minutes

**Number of servings:** 4

**Ingredients:**

- 1 tablespoon olive oil
- 1 onion, diced
- 2 cloves garlic, minced
- 4 cups broccoli florets
- 3 cups vegetable broth
- 1 can (13.5 ounces) coconut milk
- Salt and pepper to taste
- Red pepper flakes for garnish (optional)

**Directions:**

1. In a large pot, heat the olive oil over medium heat. Add the diced onion and cook until softened, about 5 minutes.
2. Add the minced garlic to the pot and cook for another 2 minutes.

3. Add the broccoli florets and vegetable broth to the pot. Bring to a boil, then reduce the heat to low and simmer for 15 minutes, or until the broccoli is tender.
4. Using an immersion blender or regular blender, puree the soup until smooth.
5. Return the soup to the pot and stir in the coconut milk. Season with salt and pepper to taste.
6. Heat the soup gently until warmed through. Serve hot, garnished with red pepper flakes if desired. Enjoy!

**Nutritional info:**

- Calories per serving: 280
- Total fat: 23g

- Cholesterol: 0mg
- Sodium: 700mg
- Total carbohydrates: 18g
- Dietary fiber: 5g
- Sugars: 3g
- Protein: 5g

**Tomato Basil Soup**

**Description:** A classic and comforting soup made with ripe tomatoes, fragrant basil, and a hint of garlic.

**Preparation time:** 10 minutes

**Cooking time:** 30 minutes

**Number of servings:** 4

**Ingredients:**

- 1 tablespoon olive oil
- 1 onion, diced
- 2 cloves garlic, minced
- 4 cups ripe tomatoes, diced (or 1 can (28 ounces) diced tomatoes)
- 2 cups vegetable broth
- 1/4 cup chopped fresh basil
- Salt and pepper to taste
- 1/4 cup heavy cream or coconut cream (optional)
- Fresh basil leaves for garnish (optional)

**Directions:**

1. In a large pot, heat the olive oil over medium heat. Add the diced onion and cook until softened, about 5 minutes.
2. Add the minced garlic to the pot and cook for another 2 minutes.
3. Add the diced tomatoes and vegetable broth to the pot. Bring to a boil, then reduce the heat to low and simmer for 20 minutes.
4. Stir in the chopped fresh basil and season with salt and pepper to taste.
5. Using an immersion blender or regular blender, puree the soup until smooth.
6. If using, stir in the heavy cream or coconut cream to add creaminess to the soup.

7. Heat the soup gently until warmed through. Serve hot, garnished with fresh basil leaves if desired. Enjoy!

**Nutritional info:**

- Calories per serving: 120
- Total fat: 5g
- Cholesterol: 0mg
- Sodium: 700mg
- Total carbohydrates: 17g
- Dietary fiber: 4g
- Sugars: 9g
- Protein: 3g

**Vegetable Noodle Soup**

**Description:** A comforting and wholesome soup filled with colorful vegetables and hearty noodles.

**Preparation time:** 15 minutes

**Cooking time:** 20 minutes

**Number of servings:** 6

**Ingredients:**

- 1 tablespoon olive oil
- 1 onion, diced
- 2 carrots, diced
- 2 celery stalks, diced
- 4 cups vegetable broth
- 2 cups water
- 1 cup diced tomatoes (fresh or canned)

- 1 cup chopped green beans
- 1 cup diced zucchini
- 1 cup cooked noodles (such as spaghetti or rotini)
- 2 tablespoons chopped fresh parsley
- Salt and pepper to taste

**Directions:**

1. In a large pot, heat the olive oil over medium heat. Add the diced onion, carrots, and celery. Cook until softened, about 5 minutes.
2. Add the vegetable broth, water, diced tomatoes, green beans, and diced zucchini to the pot. Bring to a boil, then reduce the heat to low and simmer for 15 minutes.

3. Stir in the cooked noodles and chopped fresh parsley. Season with salt and pepper to taste.
4. Simmer for another 5 minutes to heat the noodles through. Serve hot and enjoy this comforting soup!

**Nutritional info:**

- Calories per serving: 150
- Total fat: 3g
- Cholesterol: 0mg
- Sodium: 600mg
- Total carbohydrates: 25g
- Dietary fiber: 5g
- Sugars: 7g
- Protein: 4g

## Black Bean Soup

**Description:** A rich and flavorful soup made with black beans, vegetables, and a blend of spices.

**Preparation time:** 15 minutes

**Cooking time:** 30 minutes

**Number of servings:** 6

**Ingredients:**

- 1 tablespoon olive oil
- 1 onion, diced
- 2 cloves garlic, minced
- 2 carrots, diced
- 2 celery stalks, diced

- 2 cans (15 ounces each) black beans, drained and rinsed
- 4 cups vegetable broth
- 1 can (14.5 ounces) diced tomatoes
- 1 teaspoon ground cumin
- 1 teaspoon chili powder
- 1/2 teaspoon smoked paprika
- Salt and pepper to taste
- Fresh cilantro for garnish (optional)
- Sour cream or avocado slices for serving (optional)

**Directions:**

1. In a large pot, heat the olive oil over medium heat. Add the diced onion and cook until softened, about 5 minutes.

2. Add the minced garlic, diced carrots, and diced celery to the pot. Cook for another 5 minutes, stirring
3. occasionally.
4. Add the drained and rinsed black beans, vegetable broth, diced tomatoes, ground cumin, chili powder, smoked paprika, salt, and pepper to the pot. Stir to combine.
5. Bring the soup to a boil, then reduce the heat to low and simmer for 20 minutes, stirring occasionally.
6. Using an immersion blender or regular blender, puree a portion of the soup to thicken it while still leaving some chunks of vegetables and beans for texture.

7. Taste and adjust seasoning if needed. Serve hot, garnished with fresh cilantro and a dollop of sour cream or slices of avocado if desired. Enjoy!

**Nutritional info:**

- Calories per serving: 220
- Total fat: 3g
- Cholesterol: 0mg
- Sodium: 800mg
- Total carbohydrates: 38g
- Dietary fiber: 12g
- Sugars: 6g
- Protein: 13g

**Avocado Lime Dressing**

**Description:** A creamy and zesty dressing made with ripe avocados and fresh lime juice, perfect for salads or as a dip.

**Preparation time:** 5 minutes

**Cooking time:** 0 minutes

**Number of servings:** Makes about 1 cup

**Ingredients:**

- 1 ripe avocado, peeled and pitted
- 1/4 cup fresh lime juice
- 2 tablespoons olive oil
- 1 clove garlic, minced
- 1/4 cup chopped fresh cilantro
- Salt and pepper to taste

**Directions:**

1. In a blender or food processor, combine the ripe avocado, fresh lime juice, olive oil, minced garlic, chopped cilantro, salt, and pepper.
2. Blend until smooth and creamy, scraping down the sides as needed to ensure everything is well incorporated.
3. Taste and adjust seasoning if needed.
4. Transfer the dressing to a jar or container with a tight-fitting lid.
5. Store in the refrigerator for up to 3 days. Shake well before using. Enjoy!

**Nutritional info:**

- Calories per serving (2 tablespoons): 60
- Total fat: 6g
- Cholesterol: 0mg

- Sodium: 5mg
- Total carbohydrates: 2g
- Dietary fiber: 1g
- Sugars: 0g
- Protein: 0g

**Cashew Ranch Dressing**

**Description:** A creamy and flavorful ranch dressing made with cashews, herbs, and tangy apple cider vinegar.

**Preparation time:** 10 minutes

**Cooking time:** 0 minutes

**Number of servings:** Makes about 1 cup

**Ingredients:**

- 1 cup raw cashews, soaked in water for at least 2 hours or overnight
- 1/2 cup water
- 2 tablespoons apple cider vinegar
- 1 tablespoon fresh lemon juice
- 1 clove garlic, minced
- 1 teaspoon onion powder
- 1 teaspoon dried dill
- 1 teaspoon dried parsley
- Salt and pepper to taste

**Directions:**

1. Drain and rinse the soaked cashews.
2. In a blender, combine the soaked cashews, water, apple cider vinegar, lemon juice, minced

garlic, onion powder, dried dill, dried parsley, salt, and pepper.

3. Blend until smooth and creamy, scraping down the sides as needed to ensure everything is well incorporated.
4. Taste and adjust seasoning if needed.
5. Transfer the dressing to a jar or container with a tight-fitting lid.
6. Store in the refrigerator for up to 5 days. Shake well before using. Enjoy!

**Nutritional info:**

- Calories per serving (2 tablespoons): 50
- Total fat: 4g
- Cholesterol: 0mg
- Sodium: 10mg

- Total carbohydrates: 3g
- Dietary fiber: 0g
- Sugars: 0g
- Protein: 2g

**Maple Mustard Vinaigrette**

**Description:** A sweet and tangy vinaigrette made with maple syrup, Dijon mustard, and apple cider vinegar.

**Preparation time:** 5 minutes

**Cooking time:** 0 minutes

**Number of servings:** Makes about 1/2 cup

**Ingredients:**

- 1/4 cup olive oil

- 2 tablespoons apple cider vinegar
- 1 tablespoon Dijon mustard
- 1 tablespoon pure maple syrup
- 1 clove garlic, minced
- Salt and pepper to taste

**Directions:**

1. In a small bowl, whisk together the olive oil, apple cider vinegar, Dijon mustard, maple syrup, minced garlic, salt, and pepper until well combined.
2. Taste and adjust seasoning if needed.
3. Transfer the vinaigrette to a jar or container with a tight-fitting lid.
4. Store in the refrigerator for up to 1 week. Shake well before using. Enjoy!

**Nutritional info:**

- Calories per serving (2 tablespoons): 120
- Total fat: 14g
- Cholesterol: 0mg
- Sodium: 60mg
- Total carbohydrates: 3g
- Dietary fiber: 0g
- Sugars: 3g
- Protein: 0g

**Crispy Baked Chickpeas**

**Description:** Crunchy and flavorful chickpeas seasoned with spices and baked until crispy, perfect for snacking or topping salads.

**Preparation time:** 5 minutes

**Cooking time:** 30 minutes

**Number of servings:** Makes about 2 cups

**Ingredients:**

- 2 cans (15 ounces each) chickpeas, drained, rinsed, and patted dry
- 2 tablespoons olive oil
- 1 teaspoon ground cumin
- 1 teaspoon smoked paprika
- 1/2 teaspoon garlic powder
- 1/2 teaspoon onion powder
- Salt and pepper to taste

**Directions:**

1. Preheat the oven to 400°F (200°C). Line a baking sheet with parchment paper.
2. In a large bowl, toss the dried chickpeas with olive oil, ground cumin, smoked paprika, garlic powder, onion powder, salt, and pepper until evenly coated.
3. Spread the seasoned chickpeas in a single layer on the prepared baking sheet.
4. Bake in the preheated oven for 25-30 minutes, stirring halfway through, until the chickpeas are crispy and golden brown.
5. Remove from the oven and let cool slightly before serving. Enjoy as a snack or as a crunchy topping for salads and soups!

**Nutritional info:**

- Calories per serving (1/4 cup): 120

- Total fat: 5g
- Cholesterol: 0mg
- Sodium: 150mg
- Total carbohydrates: 14g
- Dietary fiber: 4g
- Sugars: 0g
- Protein: 5g

**Coconut Bacon Bits**

**Description:** Crispy and smoky coconut flakes seasoned with maple syrup and smoked paprika, perfect for adding a savory crunch to salads, soups, and more.

**Preparation time:** 5 minutes

**Cooking time:** 15 minutes

**Number of servings:** Makes about 1 cup

**Ingredients:**

- 1 cup unsweetened coconut flakes
- 1 tablespoon soy sauce or tamari
- 1 tablespoon maple syrup
- 1/2 teaspoon smoked paprika
- 1/4 teaspoon garlic powder
- 1/4 teaspoon onion powder

**Directions:**

1. Preheat the oven to 325°F (160°C). Line a baking sheet with parchment paper.
2. In a bowl, combine the unsweetened coconut flakes, soy sauce or tamari, maple syrup,

smoked paprika, garlic powder, and onion powder. Toss until the coconut flakes are evenly coated.

3. Spread the seasoned coconut flakes in an even layer on the prepared baking sheet.
4. Bake in the preheated oven for 10-15 minutes, stirring occasionally, until the coconut flakes are crispy and golden brown.
5. Remove from the oven and let cool completely before serving or storing in an airtight container. Enjoy as a vegan alternative to bacon bits!

**Nutritional info:**

- Calories per serving (2 tablespoons): 60
- Total fat: 5g

- Cholesterol: 0mg
- Sodium: 80mg
- Total carbohydrates: 4g
- Dietary fiber: 2g
- Sugars: 2g
- Protein: 1g

**Quinoa Tabbouleh Salad**

**Description:** A refreshing twist on traditional tabbouleh salad, featuring quinoa instead of bulgur for added protein and texture.

**Preparation time:** 15 minutes

**Cooking time:** 15 minutes

**Number of servings:** 4

**Ingredients:**

- 1 cup quinoa, rinsed
- 2 cups water
- 1 cup chopped cucumber
- 1 cup chopped tomatoes
- 1/2 cup chopped fresh parsley
- 1/4 cup chopped fresh mint
- 1/4 cup diced red onion
- 2 tablespoons olive oil
- 2 tablespoons fresh lemon juice
- Salt and pepper to taste

**Directions:**

1. In a medium saucepan, bring the water to a boil. Add the rinsed quinoa, reduce heat to low,

cover, and simmer for 15 minutes, or until all the water is absorbed and the quinoa is tender.

2. Fluff the cooked quinoa with a fork and let it cool to room temperature.
3. In a large bowl, combine the cooked quinoa, chopped cucumber, chopped tomatoes, chopped parsley, chopped mint, and diced red onion.
4. In a small bowl, whisk together the olive oil, fresh lemon juice, salt, and pepper to make the dressing.
5. Pour the dressing over the salad ingredients and toss until everything is well coated.
6. Taste and adjust seasoning if needed. Serve chilled or at room temperature. Enjoy!

**Nutritional info:**

- Calories per serving: 220
- Total fat: 8g
- Cholesterol: 0mg
- Sodium: 10mg
- Total carbohydrates: 31g
- Dietary fiber: 4g
- Sugars: 2g
- Protein: 6g

**Cucumber and Dill Salad**

**Description:** A light and refreshing salad featuring crisp cucumber slices tossed with tangy yogurt and fresh dill.

**Preparation time:** 10 minutes

**Cooking time:** 0 minutes

**Number of servings:** 4

**Ingredients:**

- 2 cucumbers, thinly sliced
- 1/2 cup plain Greek yogurt
- 2 tablespoons chopped fresh dill
- 1 tablespoon lemon juice
- Salt and pepper to taste

**Directions:**

1. In a large bowl, combine the thinly sliced cucumbers, plain Greek yogurt, chopped fresh dill, lemon juice, salt, and pepper.
2. Toss until the cucumber slices are evenly coated with the yogurt mixture.

3. Taste and adjust seasoning if needed.
4. Serve chilled as a refreshing side dish or topping for grilled meats. Enjoy!

**Nutritional info:**

- Calories per serving: 30
- Total fat: 0g
- Cholesterol: 0mg
- Sodium: 15mg
- Total carbohydrates: 5g
- Dietary fiber: 1g
- Sugars: 3g
- Protein: 2g

**Moroccan Carrot Salad**

**Description:** A vibrant and flavorful salad featuring shredded carrots tossed with aromatic spices, raisins, and a tangy dressing.

**Preparation time:** 15 minutes

**Cooking time:** 0 minutes

**Number of servings:** 4

**Ingredients:**

- 4 cups shredded carrots
- 1/4 cup raisins
- 2 tablespoons chopped fresh parsley
- 2 tablespoons lemon juice
- 1 tablespoon olive oil
- 1 teaspoon ground cumin
- 1/2 teaspoon ground cinnamon

- 1/4 teaspoon ground ginger
- Salt and pepper to taste

**Directions:**

1. In a large bowl, combine the shredded carrots, raisins, chopped fresh parsley, lemon juice, olive oil, ground cumin, ground cinnamon, ground ginger, salt, and pepper.
2. Toss until the carrots are evenly coated with the dressing and spices.
3. Taste and adjust seasoning if needed.
4. Serve chilled or at room temperature as a colorful and flavorful side dish. Enjoy!

**Nutritional info:**

- Calories per serving: 90
- Total fat: 3g

- Cholesterol: 0mg
- Sodium: 60mg
- Total carbohydrates: 16g
- Dietary fiber: 4g
- Sugars: 9g
- Protein: 1g

**Edamame and Corn Salad**

**Description:** A protein-packed salad featuring edamame, sweet corn, crunchy bell peppers, and a tangy lime dressing.

**Preparation time:** 10 minutes

**Cooking time:** 5 minutes

**Number of servings:** 4

**Ingredients:**

- 1 cup shelled edamame
- 1 cup sweet corn kernels (fresh or frozen)
- 1 bell pepper, diced (any color)
- 2 green onions, thinly sliced
- 2 tablespoons chopped fresh cilantro
- 2 tablespoons lime juice
- 1 tablespoon olive oil
- 1 teaspoon honey or maple syrup
- Salt and pepper to taste

**Directions:**

1. Bring a pot of water to a boil. Add the shelled edamame and sweet corn kernels and cook for 3-5 minutes, or until tender. Drain and rinse under cold water to cool.

2. In a large bowl, combine the cooked edamame, sweet corn kernels, diced bell pepper, sliced green onions, and chopped fresh cilantro.
3. In a small bowl, whisk together the lime juice, olive oil, honey or maple syrup, salt, and pepper to make the dressing.
4. Pour the dressing over the salad ingredients and toss until everything is well coated.
5. Taste and adjust seasoning if needed. Serve chilled or at room temperature. Enjoy!

**Nutritional info:**

- Calories per serving: 130
- Total fat: 5g
- Cholesterol: 0mg
- Sodium: 20mg

- Total carbohydrates: 18g
- Dietary fiber: 4g
- Sugars: 6g
- Protein: 5g

**Watermelon Feta Salad (with vegan feta)**

**Description:** A refreshing and summery salad featuring juicy watermelon cubes, tangy vegan feta cheese, and fresh mint.

**Preparation time:** 10 minutes

**Cooking time:** 0 minutes

**Number of servings:** 4

**Ingredients:**

- 4 cups cubed watermelon

- 1/2 cup crumbled vegan feta cheese
- 2 tablespoons chopped fresh mint leaves
- 1 tablespoon balsamic vinegar (optional)
- Salt and pepper to taste

**Directions:**

1. In a large bowl, combine the cubed watermelon, crumbled vegan feta cheese, and chopped fresh mint leaves.
2. If desired, drizzle balsamic vinegar over the salad for added flavor.
3. Toss gently until everything is evenly mixed.
4. Taste and adjust seasoning if needed.
5. Serve immediately as a refreshing side dish or appetizer. Enjoy the sweet and savory flavors!

**Nutritional info:**

- Calories per serving: 90
- Total fat: 2g
- Cholesterol: 0mg
- Sodium: 180mg
- Total carbohydrates: 20g
- Dietary fiber: 1g
- Sugars: 16g
- Protein: 1g

**Curried Cauliflower Soup**

**Description:** A creamy and flavorful soup infused with aromatic curry spices and roasted cauliflower.

**Preparation time:** 15 minutes

**Cooking time:** 35 minutes

**Number of servings:** 4

**Ingredients:**

- 1 head cauliflower, cut into florets
- 2 tablespoons olive oil
- 1 onion, diced
- 2 cloves garlic, minced
- 1 tablespoon curry powder
- 1 teaspoon ground cumin
- 1/2 teaspoon ground turmeric
- 4 cups vegetable broth
- 1 cup coconut milk
- Salt and pepper to taste
- Fresh cilantro for garnish (optional)

**Directions:**

1. Preheat the oven to 400°F (200°C). Place the cauliflower florets on a baking sheet, drizzle with olive oil, and season with salt and pepper. Roast in the oven for 25-30 minutes, or until golden brown and tender.
2. In a large pot, heat the olive oil over medium heat. Add the diced onion and cook until softened, about 5 minutes.
3. Add the minced garlic, curry powder, ground cumin, and ground turmeric to the pot. Cook for another 2 minutes, stirring constantly.
4. Add the roasted cauliflower florets and vegetable broth to the pot. Bring to a boil, then reduce the heat to low and simmer for 10 minutes.

5. Use an immersion blender or regular blender to puree the soup until smooth and creamy.
6. Stir in the coconut milk and heat gently until warmed through.
7. Taste and adjust seasoning if needed. Serve hot, garnished with fresh cilantro if desired. Enjoy the fragrant flavors of this curried cauliflower soup!

**Nutritional info:**

- Calories per serving: 200
- Total fat: 15g
- Cholesterol: 0mg
- Sodium: 700mg
- Total carbohydrates: 15g
- Dietary fiber: 5g

- Sugars: 5g
- Protein: 5g

### Vegetarian Chili

**Description:** A hearty and satisfying chili packed with beans, vegetables, and bold spices, perfect for a cozy meal.

**Preparation time:** 15 minutes

**Cooking time:** 30 minutes

**Number of servings:** 6

**Ingredients:**

- 1 tablespoon olive oil
- 1 onion, diced
- 2 cloves garlic, minced

- 1 bell pepper, diced (any color)
- 1 zucchini, diced
- 1 cup corn kernels (fresh or frozen)
- 1 can (15 ounces) black beans, drained and rinsed
- 1 can (15 ounces) kidney beans, drained and rinsed
- 1 can (15 ounces) diced tomatoes
- 2 cups vegetable broth
- 2 tablespoons chili powder
- 1 teaspoon ground cumin
- 1 teaspoon smoked paprika
- Salt and pepper to taste
- Fresh cilantro for garnish (optional)
- Avocado slices for serving (optional)

**Directions:**

1. In a large pot, heat the olive oil over medium heat. Add the diced onion and cook until softened, about 5 minutes.
2. Add the minced garlic, diced bell pepper, and diced zucchini to the pot. Cook for another 5 minutes, stirring occasionally.
3. Stir in the corn kernels, black beans, kidney beans, diced tomatoes (with their juices), vegetable broth, chili powder, ground cumin, smoked paprika, salt, and pepper.
4. Bring the chili to a boil, then reduce the heat to low and simmer for 20-25 minutes, stirring occasionally, until the vegetables are tender and the flavors have melded together.
5. Taste and adjust seasoning if needed.

6. Serve hot, garnished with fresh cilantro and avocado slices if desired. Enjoy this comforting vegetarian chili!

**Nutritional info:**

- Calories per serving: 250
- Total fat: 3g
- Cholesterol: 0mg
- Sodium: 600mg
- Total carbohydrates: 45g
- Dietary fiber: 12g
- Sugars: 7g
- Protein: 13g

**Minestrone Soup**

**Description:** A classic Italian soup featuring a hearty mix of vegetables, beans, pasta, and savory broth.

**Preparation time:** 15 minutes

**Cooking time:** 30 minutes

**Number of servings:** 6

**Ingredients:**

- 1 tablespoon olive oil
- 1 onion, diced
- 2 cloves garlic, minced
- 2 carrots, diced
- 2 celery stalks, diced
- 1 zucchini, diced

- 1 cup green beans, trimmed and cut into bite-sized pieces
- 1 can (15 ounces) diced tomatoes
- 6 cups vegetable broth
- 1 can (15 ounces) kidney beans, drained and rinsed
- 1/2 cup small pasta (such as ditalini or elbow)
- 2 tablespoons chopped fresh basil
- Salt and pepper to taste
- Grated Parmesan cheese for serving (optional)

**Directions:**

1. In a large pot, heat the olive oil over medium heat. Add the diced onion and cook until softened, about 5 minutes.

2. Add the minced garlic, diced carrots, diced celery, diced zucchini, and green beans to the pot. Cook for another 5 minutes, stirring occasionally.
3. Stir in the diced tomatoes (with their juices), vegetable broth, kidney beans, and small pasta. Bring the soup to a boil.
4. Reduce the heat to low and simmer for 20-25 minutes, or until the vegetables are tender and the pasta is cooked through.
5. Stir in the chopped fresh basil and season with salt and pepper to taste.
6. Serve hot, garnished with grated Parmesan cheese if desired. Enjoy this comforting and nutritious minestrone soup!

**Nutritional info:**

- Calories per serving: 200
- Total fat: 2g
- Cholesterol: 0mg
- Sodium: 700mg
- Total carbohydrates: 40g
- Dietary fiber: 9g
- Sugars: 8g
- Protein: 9g

**Red Lentil Soup**

**Description:** A hearty and comforting soup made with red lentils, vegetables, and warming spices.

**Preparation time:** 10 minutes

**Cooking time:** 25 minutes

**Number of servings:** 4

**Ingredients:**

- 1 tablespoon olive oil
- 1 onion, diced
- 2 cloves garlic, minced
- 2 carrots, diced
- 2 celery stalks, diced
- 1 cup red lentils, rinsed
- 4 cups vegetable broth
- 1 teaspoon ground cumin
- 1/2 teaspoon ground turmeric
- 1/2 teaspoon ground coriander
- 1/4 teaspoon cayenne pepper (optional)

- Salt and pepper to taste
- Fresh cilantro for garnish (optional)
- Lemon wedges for serving (optional)

**Directions:**

1. In a large pot, heat the olive oil over medium heat. Add the diced onion and cook until softened, about 5 minutes.
2. Add the minced garlic, diced carrots, and diced celery to the pot. Cook for another 5 minutes, stirring occasionally.
3. Stir in the red lentils, vegetable broth, ground cumin, ground turmeric, ground coriander, and cayenne pepper (if using).
4. Bring the soup to a boil, then reduce the heat to low and simmer for 15-20 minutes, or until

the lentils are tender and the soup has thickened.

5. Taste and adjust seasoning if needed.
6. Serve hot, garnished with fresh cilantro and lemon wedges if desired. Enjoy this nourishing and flavorful red lentil soup!

**Nutritional info:**

- Calories per serving: 220
- Total fat: 3g
- Cholesterol: 0mg
- Sodium: 800mg
- Total carbohydrates: 36g
- Dietary fiber: 12g
- Sugars: 5g
- Protein: 13g

**Butternut Squash Soup**

**Description:** A velvety and creamy soup made with roasted butternut squash, aromatic spices, and a hint of sweetness.

**Preparation time:** 15 minutes

**Cooking time:** 45 minutes

**Number of servings:** 4

**Ingredients:**

- 1 butternut squash, peeled, seeded, and diced
- 2 tablespoons olive oil
- 1 onion, diced
- 2 cloves garlic, minced
- 4 cups vegetable broth

- 1 teaspoon ground cinnamon
- 1/2 teaspoon ground nutmeg
- 1/4 teaspoon ground ginger
- Salt and pepper to taste
- Coconut milk or cream for garnish (optional)
- Toasted pumpkin seeds for garnish (optional)

**Directions:**

1. Preheat the oven to 400°F (200°C). Place the diced butternut squash on a baking sheet, drizzle with olive oil, and season with salt and pepper. Roast in the oven for 25-30 minutes, or until tender and caramelized.
2. In a large pot, heat the olive oil over medium heat. Add the diced onion and cook until softened, about 5 minutes.

3. Add the minced garlic to the pot and cook for another 2 minutes.
4. Add the roasted butternut squash, vegetable broth, ground cinnamon, ground nutmeg, and ground ginger to the pot. Bring to a boil, then reduce the heat to low and simmer for 15-20 minutes.
5. Use an immersion blender or regular blender to puree the soup until smooth and creamy.
6. Taste and adjust seasoning if needed.
7. Serve hot, garnished with a swirl of coconut milk or cream and toasted pumpkin seeds if desired. Enjoy the rich and comforting flavors of this butternut squash soup!

**Nutritional info:**

- Calories per serving: 180

- Total fat: 7g
- Cholesterol: 0mg
- Sodium: 700mg
- Total carbohydrates: 28g
- Dietary fiber: 6g
- Sugars: 5g
- Protein: 3g

**Tahini Dressing**

**Description:** A creamy and nutty dressing made with tahini, lemon juice, garlic, and olive oil, perfect for salads, grain bowls, or as a dip.

**Preparation time:** 5 minutes

**Cooking time:** 0 minutes

**Number of servings:** Makes about 1 cup

**Ingredients:**

- 1/4 cup tahini
- 2 tablespoons fresh lemon juice
- 1 clove garlic, minced
- 2 tablespoons olive oil
- 2-4 tablespoons water, to thin
- Salt and pepper to taste

**Directions:**

1. In a small bowl, whisk together the tahini, fresh lemon juice, minced garlic, olive oil, salt, and pepper.
2. Gradually add water, 1 tablespoon at a time, until the desired consistency is reached. The dressing should be smooth and pourable.

3. Taste and adjust seasoning if needed.
4. Transfer the dressing to a jar or container with a tight-fitting lid.
5. Store in the refrigerator for up to 1 week. Stir well before using. Enjoy the creamy and nutty flavor of this tahini dressing!

**Nutritional info:**

- Calories per serving (2 tablespoons): 70
- Total fat: 7g
- Cholesterol: 0mg
- Sodium: 30mg
- Total carbohydrates: 2g
- Dietary fiber: 1g
- Sugars: 0g
- Protein: 1g

**Pesto Vinaigrette**

**Description:** A tangy and herbaceous vinaigrette made with homemade or store-bought pesto, olive oil, and vinegar.

**Preparation time:** 5 minutes

**Cooking time:** 0 minutes

**Number of servings:** Makes about 1/2 cup

**Ingredients:**

- 1/4 cup pesto (homemade or store-bought)
- 2 tablespoons white wine vinegar or red wine vinegar
- 1/4 cup olive oil
- Salt and pepper to taste

**Directions:**

1. In a small bowl, whisk together the pesto and vinegar until well combined.
2. Slowly drizzle in the olive oil while whisking continuously until the vinaigrette is emulsified.
3. Season with salt and pepper to taste.
4. Transfer the vinaigrette to a jar or container with a tight-fitting lid.
5. Store in the refrigerator for up to 1 week. Shake well before using. Enjoy the vibrant flavors of this pesto vinaigrette!

**Nutritional info:**

- Calories per serving (2 tablespoons): 120
- Total fat: 13g
- Cholesterol: 0mg

- Sodium: 90mg
- Total carbohydrates: 1g
- Dietary fiber: 0g
- Sugars: 0g
- Protein: 1g

**Crunchy Garlic Croutons**

**Description:** Homemade croutons seasoned with garlic and herbs, perfect for adding a crunchy topping to salads and soups.

**Preparation time:** 10 minutes

**Cooking time:** 15 minutes

**Number of servings:** Makes about 2 cups

**Ingredients:**

- 4 cups cubed bread (day-old or slightly stale)
- 2 tablespoons olive oil
- 2 cloves garlic, minced
- 1 teaspoon dried Italian herbs (such as oregano, basil, and thyme)
- Salt and pepper to taste

**Directions:**

1. Preheat the oven to 375°F (190°C). Line a baking sheet with parchment paper.
2. In a large bowl, toss the cubed bread with olive oil, minced garlic, dried Italian herbs, salt, and pepper until evenly coated.
3. Spread the seasoned bread cubes in a single layer on the prepared baking sheet.

4. Bake in the preheated oven for 12-15 minutes, stirring halfway through, until the croutons are golden brown and crispy.
5. Remove from the oven and let cool completely before serving or storing in an airtight container. Enjoy the satisfying crunch of these homemade garlic croutons!

**Nutritional info:**

- Serving size: 1/4 cup
- Calories per serving: 60
- Total fat: 3g
- Cholesterol: 0mg
- Sodium: 100mg
- Total carbohydrates: 8g
- Dietary fiber: 1g

- Sugars: 1g
- Protein: 2g

## Spicy Cashew Crumble

**Description:** A crunchy and flavorful topping made with roasted cashews, spices, and a touch of heat, perfect for sprinkling on salads, soups, or roasted vegetables.

**Preparation time:** 5 minutes

**Cooking time:** 10 minutes

**Number of servings:** Makes about 1 cup

**Ingredients:**

- 1 cup raw cashews
- 1 tablespoon olive oil

- 1 teaspoon ground cumin
- 1/2 teaspoon smoked paprika
- 1/4 teaspoon cayenne pepper
- Salt to taste

**Directions:**

1. Preheat the oven to 350°F (175°C). Line a baking sheet with parchment paper.
2. In a bowl, toss the raw cashews with olive oil, ground cumin, smoked paprika, cayenne pepper, and salt until evenly coated.
3. Spread the seasoned cashews in a single layer on the prepared baking sheet.
4. Bake in the preheated oven for 8-10 minutes, stirring halfway through, until the cashews are golden brown and fragrant.

5. Remove from the oven and let cool completely before serving or storing in an airtight container. Enjoy the spicy and crunchy goodness of this cashew crumble!

**Nutritional info:**

- Serving size: 2 tablespoons
- Calories per serving: 90
- Total fat: 8g
- Cholesterol: 0mg
- Sodium: 25mg
- Total carbohydrates: 4g
- Dietary fiber: 1g
- Sugars: 0g
- Protein: 2g

## Pickled Red Onions

**Description:** Tangy and vibrant red onions pickled in a sweet and tangy brine, perfect for adding a pop of flavor to sandwiches, salads, tacos, and more.

**Preparation time:** 10 minutes

**Cooking time:** 5 minutes (cooling time not included)

**Number of servings:** Makes about 1 cup

**Ingredients:**

- 1 large red onion, thinly sliced
- 1/2 cup apple cider vinegar
- 1/4 cup water
- 2 tablespoons granulated sugar

- 1 teaspoon salt
- 1/2 teaspoon whole black peppercorns
- 1/2 teaspoon mustard seeds

**Directions:**

1. Place the thinly sliced red onion in a clean glass jar or container with a tight-fitting lid.
2. In a small saucepan, combine the apple cider vinegar, water, granulated sugar, salt, whole black peppercorns, and mustard seeds. Bring to a boil over medium heat, stirring until the sugar and salt are dissolved.
3. Pour the hot brine over the sliced red onion in the jar, making sure the onions are completely submerged.

4. Let the pickled onions cool to room temperature, then cover with the lid and refrigerate for at least 1 hour before serving. The pickled onions will keep in the refrigerator for up to 2 weeks. Enjoy the tangy and colorful addition to your favorite dishes!

**Nutritional info:**

- Serving size: 2 tablespoons
- Calories per serving: 10
- Total fat: 0g
- Cholesterol: 0mg
- Sodium: 150mg
- Total carbohydrates: 2g
- Dietary fiber: 0g
- Sugars: 1g

- Protein: 0g

# Chapter 5

# Plant-Powered Mains

**Black Bean Veggie Burgers**

**Description:** Hearty and flavorful veggie burgers made with black beans, vegetables, and spices, perfect for a meatless burger option.

**Preparation time:** 20 minutes

**Cooking time:** 10 minutes

**Number of servings:** Makes 4 burgers

**Ingredients:**

- 1 can (15 ounces) black beans, drained and rinsed

- 1/2 cup cooked quinoa
- 1/2 cup bread crumbs
- 1/4 cup finely chopped onion
- 1/4 cup finely chopped bell pepper
- 2 cloves garlic, minced
- 1 teaspoon ground cumin
- 1 teaspoon chili powder
- Salt and pepper to taste
- 1 tablespoon olive oil (for cooking)

**Directions:**

1. In a large mixing bowl, mash the black beans with a fork or potato masher until mostly smooth, with some chunks remaining.
2. Add the cooked quinoa, bread crumbs, chopped onion, chopped bell pepper, minced

garlic, ground cumin, chili powder, salt, and pepper to the bowl. Mix until well combined.

3. Divide the mixture into 4 equal portions and shape each portion into a patty.
4. Heat olive oil in a skillet over medium heat. Cook the veggie burgers for 4-5 minutes on each side, or until golden brown and heated through.
5. Serve the black bean veggie burgers on buns with your favorite toppings and condiments. Enjoy the plant-based goodness!

**Nutritional info:**

- Calories per serving (1 burger): 220
- Total fat: 4g
- Cholesterol: 0mg

- Sodium: 380mg
- Total carbohydrates: 36g
- Dietary fiber: 10g
- Sugars: 2g
- Protein: 10g

**Lentil and Quinoa Patties**

**Description:** Nutritious and protein-packed patties made with lentils, quinoa, and savory spices, perfect for a vegetarian meal option.

**Preparation time:** 20 minutes

**Cooking time:** 20 minutes

**Number of servings:** Makes 8 patties

**Ingredients:**

- 1/2 cup uncooked quinoa
- 1 cup cooked lentils
- 1/2 cup bread crumbs
- 1/4 cup finely chopped onion
- 2 cloves garlic, minced
- 1 teaspoon ground cumin
- 1 teaspoon smoked paprika
- Salt and pepper to taste
- 2 tablespoons olive oil (for cooking)

**Directions:**

1. Cook the quinoa according to package instructions and let it cool to room temperature.
2. In a large mixing bowl, combine the cooked quinoa, cooked lentils, bread crumbs, chopped

onion, minced garlic, ground cumin, smoked paprika, salt, and pepper. Mix until well combined.

3. Divide the mixture into 8 equal portions and shape each portion into a patty.
4. Heat olive oil in a skillet over medium heat. Cook the lentil and quinoa patties for 4-5 minutes on each side, or until golden brown and heated through.
5. Serve the patties with your favorite sauces, dips, or in a burger bun with toppings. Enjoy these wholesome and satisfying vegetarian patties!

**Nutritional info:**

- Calories per serving (1 patty): 130
- Total fat: 4g

- Cholesterol: 0mg
- Sodium: 150mg
- Total carbohydrates: 18g
- Dietary fiber: 4g
- Sugars: 1g
- Protein: 6g

**Chickpea Falafel Burgers**

**Description:** Flavorful and aromatic falafel burgers made with chickpeas, herbs, and spices, perfect for a vegetarian twist on a classic burger.

**Preparation time:** 20 minutes

**Cooking time:** 15 minutes

**Number of servings:** Makes 4 burgers

**Ingredients:**

- 1 can (15 ounces) chickpeas, drained and rinsed
- 1/4 cup chopped fresh parsley
- 1/4 cup chopped fresh cilantro
- 2 cloves garlic, minced
- 1 teaspoon ground cumin
- 1 teaspoon ground coriander
- 1/2 teaspoon baking powder
- Salt and pepper to taste
- 2 tablespoons olive oil (for cooking)

**Directions:**

1. In a food processor, combine the chickpeas, chopped parsley, chopped cilantro, minced

garlic, ground cumin, ground coriander, baking powder, salt, and pepper. Pulse until the mixture comes together but still has some texture.

2. Divide the mixture into 4 equal portions and shape each portion into a patty.
3. Heat olive oil in a skillet over medium heat. Cook the falafel burgers for 3-4 minutes on each side, or until golden brown and crispy.
4. Serve the falafel burgers on buns with tzatziki sauce, lettuce, tomato, and cucumber slices. Enjoy the delicious flavors of these chickpea falafel burgers!

**Nutritional info:**

- Calories per serving (1 burger): 200
- Total fat: 8g

- Cholesterol: 0mg
- Sodium: 320mg
- Total carbohydrates: 26g
- Dietary fiber: 7g
- Sugars: 1g
- Protein: 7g

**Portobello Mushroom Burgers**

**Description:** Juicy and savory mushroom burgers made with marinated portobello mushrooms, grilled to perfection and served with your favorite toppings.

**Preparation time:** 15 minutes

**Cooking time:** 10 minutes

**Number of servings:** Makes 4 burgers

**Ingredients:**

- 4 large portobello mushroom caps
- 1/4 cup balsamic vinegar
- 2 tablespoons olive oil
- 2 cloves garlic, minced
- 1 teaspoon dried thyme
- Salt and pepper to taste
- 4 burger buns
- Toppings of your choice (lettuce, tomato, onion, avocado, etc.)

**Directions:**

1. In a shallow dish, whisk together the balsamic vinegar, olive oil, minced garlic, dried thyme, salt, and pepper to make the marinade.
2. Place the portobello mushroom caps in the marinade, turning to coat evenly. Let them marinate for 10-15 minutes.
3. Preheat the grill or grill pan over medium-high heat. Remove the mushrooms from the marinade and grill for 4-5 minutes on each side, or until tender and grill marks appear.
4. Toast the burger buns on the grill for 1-2 minutes, until lightly golden brown.
5. Assemble the portobello mushroom burgers by placing each grilled mushroom cap on a bun and topping with your favorite toppings.

6. Serve immediately and enjoy the rich and meaty flavor of these portobello mushroom burgers!

**Nutritional info:**

- Calories per serving (1 burger): 180
- Total fat: 7g
- Cholesterol: 0mg
- Sodium: 200mg
- Total carbohydrates: 25g
- Dietary fiber: 3g
- Sugars: 5g
- Protein: 5g

**Sweet Potato and Oat Patties**

**Description:** Wholesome and satisfying patties made with mashed sweet potatoes, oats, and aromatic spices, perfect for a nutritious meal option.

**Preparation time:** 20 minutes

**Cooking time:** 15 minutes

**Number of servings:** Makes 8 patties

**Ingredients:**

- 2 cups mashed sweet potatoes (about 2 medium sweet potatoes)
- 1 cup rolled oats
- 1/4 cup finely chopped onion
- 2 cloves garlic, minced
- 1 teaspoon ground cumin

- 1/2 teaspoon smoked paprika
- Salt and pepper to taste
- 2 tablespoons olive oil (for cooking)

**Directions:**

1. In a large mixing bowl, combine the mashed sweet potatoes, rolled oats, chopped onion, minced garlic, ground cumin, smoked paprika, salt, and pepper. Mix until well combined.
2. Divide the mixture into 8 equal portions and shape each portion into a patty.
3. Heat olive oil in a skillet over medium heat. Cook the sweet potato and oat patties for 4-5 minutes on each side, or until golden brown and heated through.

4. Serve the patties with your favorite sauces, dips, or on a bed of greens. Enjoy these wholesome and flavorful sweet potato and oat patties!

**Nutritional info:**

- Calories per serving (1 patty): 120
- Total fat: 3g
- Cholesterol: 0mg
- Sodium: 120mg
- Total carbohydrates: 20g
- Dietary fiber: 3g
- Sugars: 3g
- Protein: 3g

**Teriyaki Tofu Buddha Bowl**

**Description:** A nourishing and flavorful Buddha bowl featuring marinated tofu, roasted vegetables, and brown rice, drizzled with homemade teriyaki sauce.

**Preparation time:** 20 minutes

**Cooking time:** 30 minutes

**Number of servings:** Makes 4 bowls

**Ingredients:**

For the teriyaki tofu:

- 1 block (14 ounces) extra-firm tofu, pressed and cubed
- 1/4 cup soy sauce (or tamari for gluten-free)
- 2 tablespoons rice vinegar
- 2 tablespoons maple syrup

- 1 clove garlic, minced
- 1 teaspoon grated ginger
- 1 teaspoon cornstarch (optional, for thickening)

For the roasted vegetables:

- 2 cups chopped mixed vegetables (such as bell peppers, broccoli, carrots, and zucchini)
- 1 tablespoon olive oil
- Salt and pepper to taste

For the bowls:

- 2 cups cooked brown rice
- Sesame seeds for garnish
- Sliced green onions for garnish

**Directions:**

1. Preheat the oven to 400°F (200°C). Line a baking sheet with parchment paper.
2. In a bowl, whisk together the soy sauce, rice vinegar, maple syrup, minced garlic, and grated ginger to make the teriyaki marinade. Add the cubed tofu and let it marinate for 15-20 minutes.
3. Arrange the marinated tofu cubes on the prepared baking sheet, reserving the marinade. Bake in the preheated oven for 20-25 minutes, or until golden brown and crispy.
4. Meanwhile, toss the chopped mixed vegetables with olive oil, salt, and pepper on another baking sheet. Roast in the oven for 15-20 minutes, or until tender and lightly caramelized.

5. In a small saucepan, bring the reserved teriyaki marinade to a simmer. If desired, whisk in cornstarch to thicken the sauce.
6. To assemble the Buddha bowls, divide the cooked brown rice among 4 bowls. Top with roasted vegetables and baked tofu cubes. Drizzle with teriyaki sauce and sprinkle with sesame seeds and sliced green onions.
7. Serve immediately and enjoy the delicious flavors of this teriyaki tofu Buddha bowl!

**Nutritional info:**

- Calories per serving (1 bowl): 350
- Total fat: 8g
- Cholesterol: 0mg
- Sodium: 600mg

- Total carbohydrates: 52g
- Dietary fiber: 6g
- Sugars: 9g
- Protein: 18g

**Mediterranean Grain Bowl**

**Description:** A vibrant and wholesome grain bowl featuring Mediterranean-inspired ingredients like chickpeas, roasted vegetables, olives, and feta cheese.

**Preparation time:** 20 minutes

**Cooking time:** 30 minutes

**Number of servings:** Makes 4 bowls

**Ingredients:**

For the roasted vegetables:

- 2 cups chopped mixed vegetables (such as bell peppers, cherry tomatoes, red onion, and zucchini)
- 1 tablespoon olive oil
- 1 teaspoon dried oregano
- Salt and pepper to taste

For the grain base:

- 2 cups cooked quinoa
- 1 can (15 ounces) chickpeas, drained and rinsed
- 1/4 cup chopped fresh parsley
- 2 tablespoons lemon juice
- 2 tablespoons extra-virgin olive oil
- Salt and pepper to taste

For the toppings:

- 1/2 cup sliced Kalamata olives
- 1/4 cup crumbled feta cheese
- Lemon wedges for serving (optional)

**Directions:**

1. Preheat the oven to 400°F (200°C). Line a baking sheet with parchment paper.
2. In a bowl, toss the chopped mixed vegetables with olive oil, dried oregano, salt, and pepper until evenly coated. Spread them out on the prepared baking sheet.
3. Roast the vegetables in the preheated oven for 20-25 minutes, or until tender and lightly caramelized.
4. In a large mixing bowl, combine the cooked quinoa, chickpeas, chopped fresh parsley,

lemon juice, extra-virgin olive oil, salt, and pepper. Mix until well combined.

5. To assemble the grain bowls, divide the quinoa and chickpea mixture among 4 bowls. Top each bowl with roasted vegetables, sliced Kalamata olives, and crumbled feta cheese.
6. Serve the Mediterranean grain bowls with lemon wedges on the side for squeezing over the top, if desired.
7. Enjoy the vibrant flavors and wholesome ingredients of this Mediterranean-inspired grain bowl!

**Nutritional info:**

- Calories per serving (1 bowl): 350
- Total fat: 14g

- Cholesterol: 5mg
- Sodium: 450mg
- Total carbohydrates: 45g
- Dietary fiber: 10g
- Sugars: 3g
- Protein: 13g

**Mexican Quinoa Bowl**

**Description:** A colorful and satisfying quinoa bowl featuring Mexican-inspired ingredients like black beans, corn, avocado, salsa, and creamy lime dressing.

**Preparation time:** 20 minutes

**Cooking time:** 20 minutes

**Number of servings:** Makes 4 bowls

**Ingredients:**

For the quinoa:

- 1 cup quinoa, rinsed
- 2 cups vegetable broth
- 1 teaspoon ground cumin
- 1/2 teaspoon chili powder
- Salt to taste

For the black beans:

- 1 can (15 ounces) black beans, drained and rinsed
- 1/2 teaspoon ground cumin
- 1/4 teaspoon chili powder
- Salt to taste

For the creamy lime dressing:

- 1/4 cup plain Greek yogurt
- 2 tablespoons fresh lime juice
- 1 tablespoon chopped fresh cilantro
- 1 clove garlic, minced
- Salt and pepper to taste

For the toppings:

- 1 cup cooked corn kernels
- 1 ripe avocado, sliced
- 1/2 cup salsa
- Lime wedges for serving (optional)

**Directions:**

1. In a saucepan, combine the rinsed quinoa, vegetable broth, ground cumin, chili powder,

and salt. Bring to a boil, then reduce the heat to low, cover, and simmer for 15-20 minutes, or until the quinoa is cooked and the liquid is absorbed.

2. In another saucepan, heat the black beans with ground cumin, chili powder, and salt until warmed through.
3. In a small bowl, whisk together the plain Greek yogurt, fresh lime juice, chopped fresh cilantro, minced garlic, salt, and pepper to make the creamy lime dressing.
4. To assemble the quinoa bowls, divide the cooked quinoa among 4 bowls. Top each bowl with black beans, cooked corn kernels, sliced avocado, and salsa.

5. Drizzle the creamy lime dressing over the bowls just before serving.
6. Serve the Mexican quinoa bowls with lime wedges on the side for squeezing over the top, if desired.
7. Enjoy the vibrant colors and bold flavors of this Mexican-inspired quinoa bowl!

**Nutritional info:**

- Calories per serving (1 bowl): 350
- Total fat: 10g
- Cholesterol: 0mg
- Sodium: 500mg
- Total carbohydrates: 55g
- Dietary fiber: 12g
- Sugars: 4g

- Protein: 14g

### Roasted Veggie and Farro Bowl

**Description:** A hearty and nutritious bowl featuring roasted vegetables, chewy farro, creamy avocado, and a tangy balsamic vinaigrette.

**Preparation time:** 20 minutes

**Cooking time:** 30 minutes

**Number of servings:** Makes 4 bowls

**Ingredients:**

For the roasted vegetables:

- 2 cups chopped mixed vegetables (such as sweet potatoes, Brussels sprouts, and cauliflower)
- 2 tablespoons olive oil
- 1 teaspoon dried thyme
- Salt and pepper to taste

For the farro:

- 1 cup farro, rinsed
- 3 cups vegetable broth
- Salt to taste

For the toppings:

- 1 ripe avocado, sliced
- 1/4 cup chopped fresh parsley
- Balsamic vinaigrette for drizzling

**Directions:**

1. Preheat the oven to 400°F (200°C). Line a baking sheet with parchment paper.
2. In a bowl, toss the chopped mixed vegetables with olive oil, dried thyme, salt, and pepper until evenly coated. Spread them out on the prepared baking sheet.
3. Roast the vegetables in the preheated oven for 25-30 minutes, or until tender and caramelized, stirring halfway through.
4. In a saucepan, combine the rinsed farro and vegetable broth. Bring to a boil, then reduce the heat to low, cover, and simmer for 20-25 minutes, or until the farro is tender and the liquid is absorbed.
5. To assemble the bowls, divide the cooked farro among 4 bowls. Top each bowl with roasted

vegetables, sliced avocado, and chopped fresh parsley.

6. Drizzle balsamic vinaigrette over the bowls just before serving.
7. Enjoy the wholesome and comforting flavors of this roasted veggie and farro bowl!

**Nutritional info:**

- Calories per serving (1 bowl): 350
- Total fat: 14g
- Cholesterol: 0mg
- Sodium: 450mg
- Total carbohydrates: 50g
- Dietary fiber: 12g
- Sugars: 4g
- Protein: 8g

## Thai Peanut Buddha Bowl

**Description:** A vibrant and flavorful Buddha bowl featuring tofu, vegetables, and brown rice, drizzled with a creamy Thai peanut sauce.

**Preparation time:** 20 minutes

**Cooking time:** 30 minutes

**Number of servings:** Makes 4 bowls

**Ingredients:**

For the tofu:

- 1 block (14 ounces) extra-firm tofu, pressed and cubed

- 2 tablespoons soy sauce (or tamari for gluten-free)
- 1 tablespoon sesame oil
- 1 tablespoon maple syrup
- 1 clove garlic, minced
- 1 teaspoon grated ginger

For the Thai peanut sauce:

- 1/4 cup creamy peanut butter
- 2 tablespoons soy sauce (or tamari for gluten-free)
- 2 tablespoons lime juice
- 1 tablespoon maple syrup
- 1 teaspoon grated ginger
- 1 clove garlic, minced
- 2-4 tablespoons water, to thin

For the bowls:

- 2 cups cooked brown rice
- 2 cups chopped mixed vegetables (such as bell peppers, carrots, and snap peas)
- Chopped fresh cilantro for garnish
- Chopped peanuts for garnish
- Lime wedges for serving (optional)

**Directions:**

1. Preheat the oven to 400°F (200°C). Line a baking sheet with parchment paper.
2. In a bowl, whisk together the soy sauce, sesame oil, maple syrup, minced garlic, and grated ginger to make the tofu marinade. Add the cubed tofu and let it marinate for 15-20 minutes.

3. Arrange the marinated tofu cubes on the prepared baking sheet. Bake in the preheated oven for 25-30 minutes, or until golden brown and crispy.
4. Meanwhile, prepare the Thai peanut sauce. In a small bowl, whisk together the creamy peanut butter, soy sauce, lime juice, maple syrup, grated ginger, minced garlic, and water until smooth and creamy. Add more water as needed to achieve the desired consistency.
5. Cook the brown rice according to package instructions.
6. In a skillet, sauté the chopped mixed vegetables until tender-crisp.
7. To assemble the Buddha bowls, divide the cooked brown rice among 4 bowls. Top each

bowl with roasted tofu, sautéed vegetables, and a generous drizzle of Thai peanut sauce.

8. Garnish with chopped fresh cilantro and chopped peanuts. Serve with lime wedges on the side for squeezing over the top, if desired.
9. Enjoy the vibrant flavors and creamy texture of this Thai peanut Buddha bowl!

**Nutritional info:**

- Calories per serving (1 bowl): 400
- Total fat: 16g
- Cholesterol: 0mg
- Sodium: 600mg
- Total carbohydrates: 52g
- Dietary fiber: 8g
- Sugars: 8g

- Protein: 16g

**Vegan Bolognese with Lentils**

**Description:** A hearty and satisfying vegan version of classic Bolognese sauce made with lentils, tomatoes, and aromatic herbs, served over pasta.

**Preparation time:** 15 minutes

**Cooking time:** 45 minutes

**Number of servings:** Makes 4 servings

**Ingredients:**

- 1 tablespoon olive oil
- 1 onion, finely chopped
- 2 cloves garlic, minced

- 1 carrot, finely chopped
- 1 celery stalk, finely chopped
- 1 cup dried green or brown lentils, rinsed and drained
- 1 can (14 ounces) crushed tomatoes
- 1 tablespoon tomato paste
- 1 teaspoon dried oregano
- 1 teaspoon dried basil
- Salt and pepper to taste
- Cooked pasta, for serving
- Chopped fresh parsley for garnish

**Directions:**

1. Heat olive oil in a large skillet over medium heat. Add the chopped onion, minced garlic, chopped carrot, and chopped celery. Sauté for

5-7 minutes, or until the vegetables are softened.

2. Add the rinsed and drained lentils to the skillet, along with the crushed tomatoes, tomato paste, dried oregano, dried basil, salt, and pepper. Stir to combine.
3. Bring the mixture to a simmer, then reduce the heat to low. Cover and cook for 30-40 minutes, stirring occasionally, until the lentils are tender and the sauce has thickened.
4. Taste and adjust seasoning if needed. If the sauce becomes too thick, you can thin it out with a little water.
5. Serve the vegan Bolognese sauce over cooked pasta, garnished with chopped fresh parsley.

6. Enjoy the rich and comforting flavors of this vegan twist on a classic Italian dish!

**Nutritional info:**

- Calories per serving (1 serving without pasta): 220
- Total fat: 3g
- Cholesterol: 0mg
- Sodium: 400mg
- Total carbohydrates: 38g
- Dietary fiber: 10g
- Sugars: 6g
- Protein: 12g

**Peanut Noodles with Crispy Tofu**

**Description:** A delicious and satisfying dish featuring tender noodles tossed in a creamy peanut sauce, topped with crispy tofu and chopped peanuts.

**Preparation time:** 20 minutes

**Cooking time:** 30 minutes

**Number of servings:** Makes 4 servings

**Ingredients:**

For the crispy tofu:

- 1 block (14 ounces) extra-firm tofu, pressed and cubed
- 2 tablespoons soy sauce (or tamari for gluten-free)
- 1 tablespoon cornstarch

- 1 tablespoon sesame oil

For the peanut noodles:

- 8 ounces (about 225g) dried noodles (such as spaghetti or linguine)
- 1/4 cup creamy peanut butter
- 2 tablespoons soy sauce (or tamari for gluten-free)
- 2 tablespoons rice vinegar
- 1 tablespoon maple syrup
- 1 clove garlic, minced
- 1 teaspoon grated ginger
- 1/4 teaspoon red pepper flakes (optional)
- 2-4 tablespoons water, to thin
- Chopped peanuts for garnish
- Chopped green onions for garnish

**Directions:**

1. Preheat the oven to 400°F (200°C). Line a baking sheet with parchment paper.
2. In a bowl, toss the cubed tofu with soy sauce and cornstarch until evenly coated.
3. Arrange the tofu cubes on the prepared baking sheet. Bake in the preheated oven for 25-30 minutes, or until golden brown and crispy.
4. Cook the noodles according to package instructions. Drain and set aside.
5. In a small bowl, whisk together the creamy peanut butter, soy sauce, rice vinegar, maple syrup, minced garlic, grated ginger, and red pepper flakes (if using). Add water, 1 tablespoon at a time, until the sauce reaches the desired consistency.

6. Toss the cooked noodles with the peanut sauce until evenly coated.
7. To serve, divide the peanut noodles among 4 plates or bowls. Top each serving with crispy tofu cubes, chopped peanuts, and chopped green onions.
8. Enjoy the creamy texture and bold flavors of these peanut noodles with crispy tofu!

**Nutritional info:**

- Calories per serving (1 serving): 400
- Total fat: 18g
- Cholesterol: 0mg
- Sodium: 600mg
- Total carbohydrates: 45g
- Dietary fiber: 6g

- Sugars: 7g
- Protein: 20g

# Chapter 6

# Sides and Snacks

## Roasted Brussels Sprouts with Balsamic Glaze

**Description:** Tender and caramelized roasted Brussels sprouts drizzled with a sweet and tangy balsamic glaze, perfect as a side dish or appetizer.

**Preparation time:** 10 minutes

**Cooking time:** 25 minutes

**Number of servings:** Makes 4 servings

**Ingredients:**

- 1 pound Brussels sprouts, trimmed and halved
- 2 tablespoons olive oil
- Salt and pepper to taste
- 2 tablespoons balsamic glaze

**Directions:**

1. Preheat the oven to 400°F (200°C). Line a baking sheet with parchment paper.
2. In a bowl, toss the Brussels sprouts with olive oil, salt, and pepper until evenly coated.
3. Spread the Brussels sprouts out on the prepared baking sheet in a single layer.
4. Roast in the preheated oven for 20-25 minutes, or until the Brussels sprouts are tender and caramelized, stirring halfway through.

5. Transfer the roasted Brussels sprouts to a serving platter and drizzle with balsamic glaze.
6. Serve immediately and enjoy the delicious combination of flavors in this roasted Brussels sprouts dish!

**Nutritional info:**

- Calories per serving (1 serving): 120
- Total fat: 7g
- Cholesterol: 0mg
- Sodium: 80mg
- Total carbohydrates: 14g
- Dietary fiber: 4g
- Sugars: 6g
- Protein: 4g

**Roasted Cauliflower with Tahini Sauce**

**Description:** Nutty and flavorful roasted cauliflower served with a creamy and tangy tahini sauce, a delicious and healthy side dish or appetizer.

**Preparation time:** 10 minutes

**Cooking time:** 25 minutes

**Number of servings:** Makes 4 servings

**Ingredients:**

For the roasted cauliflower:

- 1 head cauliflower, cut into florets
- 2 tablespoons olive oil
- 1 teaspoon ground cumin
- 1 teaspoon smoked paprika

- Salt and pepper to taste

For the tahini sauce:

- 1/4 cup tahini
- 2 tablespoons lemon juice
- 1 clove garlic, minced
- 2-4 tablespoons water, to thin
- Salt to taste

**Directions:**

1. Preheat the oven to 400°F (200°C). Line a baking sheet with parchment paper.
2. In a bowl, toss the cauliflower florets with olive oil, ground cumin, smoked paprika, salt, and pepper until evenly coated.
3. Spread the cauliflower out on the prepared baking sheet in a single layer.

4. Roast in the preheated oven for 20-25 minutes, or until the cauliflower is tender and golden brown, stirring halfway through.
5. Meanwhile, prepare the tahini sauce. In a small bowl, whisk together the tahini, lemon juice, minced garlic, and water until smooth and creamy. Add more water as needed to achieve the desired consistency. Season with salt to taste.
6. Serve the roasted cauliflower with the tahini sauce drizzled on top.
7. Enjoy the nutty flavor and creamy texture of this roasted cauliflower dish!

**Nutritional info:**

- Calories per serving (1 serving with sauce): 150
- Total fat: 12g

- Cholesterol: 0mg
- Sodium: 60mg
- Total carbohydrates: 10g
- Dietary fiber: 4g
- Sugars: 2g
- Protein: 4g

**Baked Sweet Potato Fries**

**Description:** Crispy and flavorful baked sweet potato fries seasoned with spices, a healthier alternative to traditional fries.

**Preparation time:** 10 minutes

**Cooking time:** 25 minutes

**Number of servings:** Makes 4 servings

**Ingredients:**

- 2 large sweet potatoes, cut into fries
- 2 tablespoons olive oil
- 1 teaspoon smoked paprika
- 1/2 teaspoon garlic powder
- 1/2 teaspoon onion powder
- Salt and pepper to taste

**Directions:**

1. Preheat the oven to 425°F (220°C). Line a baking sheet with parchment paper.
2. In a bowl, toss the sweet potato fries with olive oil, smoked paprika, garlic powder, onion powder, salt, and pepper until evenly coated.

3. Spread the sweet potato fries out on the prepared baking sheet in a single layer, making sure they are not crowded.
4. Bake in the preheated oven for 20-25 minutes, flipping halfway through, or until the fries are crispy and golden brown.
5. Remove from the oven and let cool for a few minutes before serving.
6. Serve the baked sweet potato fries hot as a delicious and nutritious snack or side dish!

**Nutritional info:**

- Calories per serving (1 serving): 150
- Total fat: 7g
- Cholesterol: 0mg
- Sodium: 150mg

- Total carbohydrates: 21g
- Dietary fiber: 3g
- Sugars: 5g
- Protein: 2g

**Roasted Vegetable Medley**

**Description:** A colorful and flavorful medley of roasted vegetables, seasoned with herbs and spices, perfect as a side dish or main course.

**Preparation time:** 10 minutes

**Cooking time:** 25 minutes

**Number of servings:** Makes 4 servings

**Ingredients:**

- 2 cups diced vegetables (such as bell peppers, zucchini, cherry tomatoes, and red onion)
- 2 tablespoons olive oil
- 1 teaspoon dried thyme
- 1 teaspoon dried rosemary
- 1/2 teaspoon garlic powder
- Salt and pepper to taste

**Directions:**

1. Preheat the oven to 425°F (220°C). Line a baking sheet with parchment paper.
2. In a bowl, toss the diced vegetables with olive oil, dried thyme, dried rosemary, garlic powder, salt, and pepper until evenly coated.
3. Spread the vegetables out on the prepared baking sheet in a single layer.

4. Roast in the preheated oven for 20-25 minutes, stirring halfway through, or until the vegetables are tender and caramelized.
5. Remove from the oven and let cool for a few minutes before serving.
6. Serve the roasted vegetable medley hot as a colorful and delicious side dish or main course!

**Nutritional info:**

- Calories per serving (1 serving): Varies depending on vegetables used
- Total fat: Varies depending on vegetables used
- Cholesterol: 0mg
- Sodium: Varies depending on vegetables used
- Total carbohydrates: Varies depending on vegetables used

- Dietary fiber: Varies depending on vegetables used
- Sugars: Varies depending on vegetables used
- Protein: Varies depending on vegetables used

**Hummus (Classic and Flavored Varieties)**

**Description:** Creamy and flavorful hummus made from chickpeas, tahini, lemon juice, garlic, and olive oil, available in classic and various flavored varieties.

**Preparation time:** 10 minutes

**Number of servings:** Makes about 2 cups

**Ingredients:**

For classic hummus:

- 1 can (15 ounces) chickpeas, drained and rinsed
- 1/4 cup tahini
- 2 tablespoons lemon juice
- 2 cloves garlic, minced
- 2 tablespoons olive oil
- Salt and pepper to taste
- Water, as needed for consistency

For flavored hummus (choose one or more):

- Roasted red pepper: 1/2 cup roasted red peppers, chopped
- Sun-dried tomato: 1/4 cup sun-dried tomatoes, soaked in hot water and drained
- Garlic and herb: 1 teaspoon dried Italian herbs, 2 cloves roasted garlic

- Spicy: 1 teaspoon ground cumin, 1/2 teaspoon smoked paprika, 1/4 teaspoon cayenne pepper

**Directions:**

1. In a food processor, combine the chickpeas, tahini, lemon juice, garlic, olive oil, salt, and pepper. Blend until smooth and creamy, scraping down the sides of the bowl as needed. If the hummus is too thick, add water, 1 tablespoon at a time, until desired consistency is reached.
2. If making flavored hummus, add the additional ingredients to the food processor and blend until well combined.
3. Transfer the hummus to a serving bowl. Drizzle with olive oil and sprinkle with paprika or fresh herbs, if desired.

4. Serve with pita bread, crackers, or fresh vegetables for dipping.
5. Enjoy the creamy texture and delicious flavor of homemade hummus!

Nutritional info (per 2 tablespoon serving):

- Calories: 70-100 (varies depending on variety)
- Total fat: 5-7g
- Cholesterol: 0mg
- Sodium: 70-150mg
- Total carbohydrates: 5-8g
- Dietary fiber: 2-3g
- Sugars: 0-1g
- Protein: 2-3g

**Baba Ghanoush (Roasted Eggplant Dip)**

**Description:** A smoky and creamy dip made from roasted eggplant, tahini, garlic, lemon juice, and olive oil, perfect for dipping or spreading on sandwiches and wraps.

**Preparation time:** 10 minutes

**Cooking time:** 30 minutes

**Number of servings:** Makes about 2 cups

**Ingredients:**

- 2 medium eggplants
- 2 tablespoons tahini
- 2 cloves garlic, minced
- 2 tablespoons lemon juice
- 2 tablespoons olive oil, plus more for drizzling
- Salt and pepper to taste

- Chopped fresh parsley for garnish

**Directions:**

1. Preheat the oven to 400°F (200°C). Line a baking sheet with parchment paper.
2. Prick the eggplants several times with a fork and place them on the prepared baking sheet. Roast in the preheated oven for 30-40 minutes, or until the eggplants are very soft and collapsed.
3. Remove the eggplants from the oven and let cool slightly. Peel off and discard the skins, then place the flesh in a colander to drain excess liquid for a few minutes.
4. In a food processor, combine the roasted eggplant flesh, tahini, minced garlic, lemon juice, olive oil, salt, and pepper. Blend until

smooth and creamy, scraping down the sides of the bowl as needed.

5. Transfer the baba ghanoush to a serving bowl. Drizzle with olive oil and sprinkle with chopped fresh parsley.
6. Serve with pita bread, crackers, or fresh vegetables for dipping.
7. Enjoy the smoky flavor and velvety texture of homemade baba ghanoush!

Nutritional info (per 2 tablespoon serving):

- Calories: 40
- Total fat: 3g
- Cholesterol: 0mg
- Sodium: 50mg
- Total carbohydrates: 4g

- Dietary fiber: 2g
- Sugars: 2g
- Protein: 1g

**White Bean and Artichoke Dip**

**Description:** A creamy and tangy dip made from white beans, artichoke hearts, garlic, lemon juice, and herbs, perfect for parties, gatherings, or as a flavorful snack.

**Preparation time:** 10 minutes

**Number of servings:** Makes about 2 cups

**Ingredients:**

- 1 can (15 ounces) white beans, drained and rinsed

- 1 can (14 ounces) artichoke hearts, drained and chopped
- 2 cloves garlic, minced
- 2 tablespoons lemon juice
- 2 tablespoons olive oil
- 2 tablespoons chopped fresh parsley
- Salt and pepper to taste

**Directions:**

1. In a food processor, combine the white beans, chopped artichoke hearts, minced garlic, lemon juice, olive oil, chopped fresh parsley, salt, and pepper. Blend until smooth and creamy, scraping down the sides of the bowl as needed.

2. If the dip is too thick, add a tablespoon of water at a time until desired consistency is reached.
3. Transfer the white bean and artichoke dip to a serving bowl.
4. Serve with crackers, breadsticks, or fresh vegetables for dipping.
5. Enjoy the creamy texture and delicious flavor of this homemade dip!

Nutritional info (per 2 tablespoon serving):

- Calories: 40
- Total fat: 2g
- Cholesterol: 0mg
- Sodium: 100mg
- Total carbohydrates: 5g

- Dietary fiber: 2g
- Sugars: 0g
- Protein: 2g

**Cashew Cheese Spread**

**Description:** A creamy and tangy cheese spread made from cashews, nutritional yeast, lemon juice, and herbs, perfect for spreading on crackers, sandwiches, or as a dip for vegetables.

**Preparation time:** 10 minutes (plus soaking time)

**Number of servings:** Makes about 1 cup

**Ingredients:**

- 1 cup raw cashews, soaked in water for at least 4 hours or overnight, drained and rinsed
- 2 tablespoons nutritional yeast
- 2 tablespoons lemon juice
- 1 clove garlic, minced
- 1/2 teaspoon salt
- 1/4 teaspoon onion powder
- 1/4 teaspoon dried thyme
- 1/4 teaspoon dried oregano
- 1/4 cup water, plus more as needed

**Directions:**

1. In a food processor or high-speed blender, combine the soaked and drained cashews, nutritional yeast, lemon juice, minced garlic,

salt, onion powder, dried thyme, and dried oregano.

2. Blend on high until smooth and creamy, scraping down the sides of the bowl as needed. Add water, 1 tablespoon at a time, until the desired consistency is reached.
3. Transfer the cashew cheese spread to a serving bowl.
4. Serve with crackers, bread, or fresh vegetables for dipping.
5. Enjoy the creamy texture and savory flavor of this homemade cashew cheese spread!

Nutritional info (per 2 tablespoon serving):

- Calories: 50
- Total fat: 4g

- Cholesterol: 0mg
- Sodium: 60mg
- Total carbohydrates: 3g
- Dietary fiber: 1g
- Sugars: 0g
- Protein: 2g

# Conclusion

As you reach the final pages of this plant-based journey, it's time to reflect on the incredible transformation that has taken place. From the moment you embarked on this culinary adventure, you've opened yourself up to a world of flavors, textures, and nourishment like never before. The plant-based realm has proven to be a feast for the senses, a celebration of nature's abundance, and a gateway to a healthier, more conscious way of living.

Throughout these pages, you've discovered the joy of crafting delectable plant-based dishes that not only delight your taste buds but also nourish your body and soul. From energizing breakfasts to hearty mains, vibrant salads to decadent desserts, you've explored the boundless possibilities of plant-based cuisine, leaving no stone unturned in your quest for flavor and satisfaction.

But this journey extends far beyond the kitchen. By embracing a plant-based lifestyle, you've taken a stand for your health, the well-being of our planet, and the ethical treatment of all living beings. Each plant-powered meal is a testament to your commitment to conscious living, a gentle reminder of the positive impact you're making with every bite.

As you turn the final page, remember that this is not the end, but rather the beginning of a lifelong adventure. The skills, knowledge, and culinary creativity you've acquired will continue to serve you well, allowing you to explore new flavors, experiment with novel ingredients, and share the joys of plant-based living with those around you.

Embrace the plant-based lifestyle with open arms, for it is a path that promises not only physical vitality but also a deep sense of joy, connection, and purpose. Let your taste buds be your guide, and let each meal be a celebration of the incredible bounty that nature has bestowed upon us.

Congratulations on taking this transformative journey, and may your plant-based odyssey continue to fill your life with vibrant flavors, radiant health, and a profound appreciation for the beauty of the plant kingdom.

Made in the USA
Monee, IL
29 July 2024

62848098R00188